THE
VIRTUE OF SEX

THE
VIRTUE OF SEX
José de Vinck

Hawthorn Books, Inc.   *Publishers*   New York

305.3
V.77
c.1

To Catherine

I will take words and mold them to your shape,
I will take sounds and curve them to your lips,
I will take rhythms and time their beat
To the throbbing of your awakened heart.
Fleet as the gull is the cry of surprise
At the surf-crested toppling of the wave;
Fleet the silken flash of half-closed eyes
And the total offering.
But I shall pluck such glories out of time,
Salvage such grace from premature death,
Bind for evermore as a sheaf of holy wheat
The treasures that we gathered, you and I.
And some young lovers, in ages yet unborn,
Looking back, perhaps, on days gone by
Will gaze upon each other in mild astonishment
And sigh:
"We were not the only lovers, you and I!"

Table of Contents

⚶ *Introduction*

> "Only this have I found, that God made man right,
> and he hath entangled himself with an infinity of
> questions."   SOLOMON

Yes, this is a dithyramb, and I admit it unashamedly. Anyone who has managed to escape from the pitfalls of self-doubt, *Weltschmerz* and manuals of moral theology will find pleasure in returning to the Dionysian groves, cleared of pagan vines and Scholastic thorns, and adorned instead with the spirit of joy.

I know only too well that in our sophisticated world a paean to sexual love runs the risk of being scorned — as if it were naïve to rejoice in a simple and good thing that has been generally destroyed, or at least falsified. Those who object to dithyrambs are the pessimists far removed from any chance of even natural salvation. This book is not for them but for others who, like my dear friend John C. H. Wu, are simple and whole enough to carry their soul on their open palm, having no reason whatsoever to blush for being in love with love.

This book has grown, as do all living things, out of an effort toward order and beauty. In the material universe, harmony is attained automatically or instinctively; in the world of man, it is the fruit of reason and free will. And yet, man is so deeply immersed in the reality of the whole creation that he partakes of it in the fullest measure.

Living man is a physical being moved by instinctive impulses

9

and performing functional acts some of which are blind while others are directed by the will. Through the constituent elements of his body, he is dependent upon the laws of physics and chemistry; through his vegetative, nutritive and reproductive functions, he is dependent upon the laws of biology; but all the while, also, in the higher regions of his being, he is a rational person dependent upon the laws of spiritual love. For love is the only logical explanation of his origin, the fundamental essence of his life and the absolute and all-satisfying end of his most vital tendencies.

Setting aside the mechanical aspects of the body, which are the concern of the physician, let us now concentrate on the object of this study: sex.

In lower animals sex is devoted to the good of the individual or species merely in the temporal order. In man, it is made to serve greater things because his final end is beyond time; he is, indeed, a biological being, but one that is called to the supreme good. In the search for a norm of life, two pitfalls may be seen: animalism, which reduces man to the lower level of instinctive gratification, and angelism, which considers him a spirit whose main function is to fight the beast. The true solution, as so often happens, may be found on the intermediate road which leads to sound realism: both aspects of man are real, and both must be made to work in harmony.

For man is indivisible, although complex. The beast he must fight, the "old man"[1] he must overcome is not the body as such, nor is it the natural instincts, but that same body and those same instincts in so far as they are vitiated by original sin.[2] He must fight, not that aspect of his physical self which shall be regenerated after death, but that unregenerated propensity of the body toward excess and disorder, and sex must become his specific means of expression of perfect human love.

Under both aspects — as a giver of life and as an act of love — the sexual power contains a mystery worthy of all respect,

[1] Cf. Rom. 6:6.
[2] Cf. Ibid. 11.

and yet too often abused. The mystery of life is defeated by
exaggerated hedonism; and the mystery of love by excess,
cruelty, irreverence, infidelity and ignorance — not to mention
the negative attitude, the crippling prejudice that appears so
often in married life itself and in the counsels addressed to
the married.

As in all vitally important matters, guidance is necessary
here, and the rules of proper conduct need to be formulated
by the magisterium of the Church. In the case of the mystery
of life, both the Church and its theologians consistently support the right of the offspring against the errors of those who
endorse the irresponsible pursuit of pleasure. As for the mystery
of married love, many authors from the Fathers down seem
to have underestimated it. For historical reasons which will
be considered later, such authors were more concerned with
correcting the failures of marriage than with exalting its sanctifying power. As an aftereffect of such mistrust, the "state of
perfection," or that of religious chastity, has long been opposed
to the "state of imperfection," or that of marital chastity. The
sacrament of matrimony has long been said to excuse concupiscence in that weaker part of humanity which did not
have the courage to practice perfect chastity. Even fairly
recent works have been leading novices to believe that the
highest mansions of heaven were reserved exclusively for
professed religious, and that their greater merit, their aureole,
was due to the fact that they had escaped from the danger
of sex.[3]

In recent years, the mystery of married love has received
closer and more sympathetic attention, and yet a complete
theology of sex remains to be written, for there is nowhere in
existence in our day an exhaustive and satisfying exposition of
the male/female relationship on the spiritual, affective and

[3] Cf. *Compendium Philosophiae Asceticae*, Adolphus a Denderwindeke,
O.F.M., Cap. (Hong Kong, 1921), pp. 116 ff.; p. 129. A revised version
of the first part of this work has been published in English under the title
Spiritual Guidance (Paterson, N.J.: St. Anthony's Guild Press, 1963).

physical planes, in so far as this relationship is willed by God and leads to him.

In presently available manuals of moral theology — at least in the Latin textbooks currently used in seminaries — the approach is neither positive nor even wholesome. These manuals are written by clerics, for clerics, in view of the defense of clerical chastity, with the intention of proving that it is the absolutely superior way of life.[4] There is a great need for corresponding treatises written by laymen, for laymen and not against them, and stressing the sacramental and sanctifying glory of the married state — with full endorsement by the Church. They must be composed by authors who know experientially what they are writing about, and who are not content to rely on outmoded concepts in defense of chastity, and do not consider Christian spouses as second-class citizens of the City of God under the pretext that the enjoyment of the full range of conjugal intimacies prevents them from rising any higher.

One of the important contributions of Pope John XXIII to the cause of truth is to have opened the windows of the Vatican to a breath of freedom in the area of theological thought. The dynamic aspects of life are now being stressed, together with the necessity of constant renewal and re-expression in contemporary style of the unchanging principles of truth. The conservative notion of static and monopolistic dogmatism is giving way to one of living progress. By freeing the theological mind from a rigidly Scholastic framework — which contained truth as perceived at a given moment of history and expressed it splendidly, but in a language often meaningless to modern man — good Pope John has encouraged further research and clarification.

We are now free to think, in all good faith and all goodwill,

---

[4] "Even in the nineteenth and twentieth centuries the minds of seminarians were shaped by moral textbooks that sounded as if they had been composed by a disgruntled St. Jerome after a particularly harrowing night of dreams of Roman maidens." *What Modern Catholics Think About Birth Control*, Daniel Sullivan (W. Birmingham, New York: Signet, 1965), p. 57.

and to express our thoughts on matters which until recently had been reserved under penalty of ecclesiastical thunder to an unapproachable and anonymous few. No longer are the contributions of laymen considered as unauthorized interferences: they are now being requested as valid means toward the effective formulation of official Church doctrine. The present work is an answer to such a request made by Cardinal Joseph Suenens of Malines-Brussels:

> Even today we hear of disagreement among moralists and the list of their variations down through the centuries is unfortunately all too long. Close contact with well informed and conscientious laymen could be a touchstone for judging whether one or another solution is actually morally and psychologically liveable. Moralists would also benefit by more closely examining human acts in the context of life's dynamism, because we run the risk of misconstruing an act's deepest motivation when we extract it from the context of life.[5]

The same open-minded attitude has been confirmed more recently in the Constitution De Ecclesia, par. 37: "They [the laity] are, by reason of the knowledge, competence or outstanding ability which they may enjoy, permitted and sometimes even obliged to express their opinion on those things which concern the good of the Church."

The most important thing, however, is not the writing of a book, but the guiding of young men and women toward truth and happiness in their personal life. Every human being in whom vitality has not slowed down to a crawling pace is immensely and justifiably interested in sex. Such universal interest needs to be fed with the strong and exhilarating food of realism. If love fails, it is often either because of the solemn rigidity of a Gothic attitude that shies away from anything lively and sensual, or on the contrary, because of the flippancy of youth that will try anything as an experience in self-

---

[5] *Love and Control* (Westminster, Md.: Newman, 1962), p. 122.

assertion, or is willing to play with sex for reasons not much deeper than that it is "fine for the complexion," to quote the author of *Lolita* in a phrase that has the ring of truth.[6]

What I am concerned with here is the personal relationship of those lovers who possess the basic requirements of happiness but may be hesitant about the proper use of their natural powers. For such as these, sexual enchantment is not paradise lost, but an oft-repeated proposition, a fruit they learn to give and receive in its own time, with tenderness and generosity, and in perfect accord with their eternal destiny.

The procreative end of marriage has been stressed with such strength and constancy that there is no great need at present to confirm it once more. This book, then, is not concerned with children. I fully accept their joyful and burdening presence as a condition of perfect marriage. I do so with such deep conviction that I presume this fact will be understood once and for all.

The problems of maladjustment and incompatibility also are not considered. We shall, however, often come across the consequences of incomprehension. As there are religious unbelievers, there are also natural unbelievers who lack faith in life and sex and happiness; who because they have failed to bring about their own harmony are wont to cast a look of doubt upon any claim of fulfillment. They are the skeptics, the cynics, the disappointed to whom any lyrical expression of love appears as childish imagination; they are also those fearful souls so heavily haunted by potential evil in the sexual act that they cannot conceive of its performance in total innocence and joy.

I venture to hope that this book will be found useful to those lovers seeking the why and the wherefore of their particular way of life. My deepest wish is to re-establish in some small measure the order and beauty of the supremely intimate expression of human love, created by God to be both orderly and beautiful.

J. de V.

[6] Vladimir Nabokov (New York: Crest), p. 126.

Part One

THE EMERGENCE OF SEX

Sex and the Historian

"O tempora, O mores!" CICERO

What has sex meant to men and women throughout the ages? The question is so vast as to be staggering, for sex, perhaps, has meant a different thing to every man and woman who ever lived. Certain patterns, however, may be seen clearly; a succession of crests and troughs, for instance, corresponding to the periods of natural optimism or pessimism. It is this cyclic motion I will now attempt to define in its broad lines, leaving the reader free to consult the many specifically historical works; for instance the American sociologist Morton M. Hunt's objective and factual study.[1]

There is no need to go into great detail or to analyze the sexual morality and practices of pre-Christian times. Suffice it to indicate that many things that were excusable on the part of unenlightened pagans are no longer acceptable in our days of greater illumination. The nature-children of earlier ages could not rise to the understanding of love in its deepest meaning, nor could they conceive the true relationship between God and sex.

Let us not imagine, however, that all pre-Christians lived

[1] *The Natural History of Love* (New York: Alfred A. Knopf, 1959).

17

in a state of depravity or promiscuity, for man left to his natural lights is perfectly able to discern the rules of a stable and moral life. Many instances are found in early writings of both East and West of the honor in which family virtues were often held. It is on the strength of such virtues that great civilizations could rise; it is in part because of their decay that they fell.

In spite of scandalous sexual abuses in Greek and Roman times, and of the frequent separation between procreation, sex and pleasure, there was in those days no trace of the two major misconceptions of our present society: the poisonous notion that sex is wicked, and the degrading view that it is purely physiological. The pagans were able to take it for what it really is on the natural level: a delightful, valuable and fully human experience. There is a tone of lighthearted happiness in much of what the Greeks and Romans wrote about love. There is often also a deep sense of the tragic which seems to be missing in the literary accounts of the epidemic affairs of our time, excepting the works of a very few authors of talent.

Ovid's *Art of Love*, in spite of being an apology of seduction, is full of delicately human touches, such as when he describes, in Book One, a first meeting of boy and girl at the stadium. The boy finds a seat next to a pretty girl, and the poet advises him: "If perchance a speck of dust falls on the young lady's lap, flick it off with your finger. And even if nothing happens to fall, with your finger flick off . . . nothing!"

The Greek farces, coarse as they may often be, are yet filled with a happy human liveliness. Both Greeks and Romans believed fully in the vital importance and joyfulness of the relationship between the sexes, and they made the most of it according to their lights. It is only in periods of decadence, and mostly among the wealthy and idle classes, that sex degenerated into vice; and, as with all civilizations, greater light was shed on the wicked than on the virtuous. In early Greece and early Rome, the worlds of Theocritus and Virgil existed in fact, running in parallel with the depraved life of the cities.

Later, the rise of Christianity coincided with the fall of Rome. As a message of meekness and purity, Christianity clashed head on with the pride and lust of the crumbling Empire. From such a conflict, the persecutions arose, followed by the period of Mediterranean expansion of the Church. It was in these unsettled times that the early Fathers — Augustine, Basil, Gregory and others — stood almost alone to fight the final agonies of a decaying world. It was then that, in their desperate search for weapons of reason against the promoters of sin, they sometimes imprudently appealed to Manichean dualism, opening a breach that is even now not completely closed.

The early forms of medieval civilization bear the mark of human love in two very different ways: the courtly and poetic on the one hand, the realistic and dramatic on the other.

Most of the earlier literary compositions of the West consisted of songs composed by roving minstrels who traveled from castle to castle: accounts of fabulous adventures of bold knights and their fair ladies, mixtures of fact and fiction, of classical and historical figures with dragons and unicorns. The tone, here, was an almost mystical sentiment of love and devotion which would lead the hero to perform incredible feats of bravery. In spite of its childishness, such a sentiment was an improvement over pagan sensuality. It helped in a way to establish the notion of a sacred relationship between man and woman and truly emphasized one of the important elements of the feminine mission: to act as the deserved object of true love, the Muse, the Egeria, the inspiration and companion of artist and king.

All minstrel songs and romances, however, were not devoted to the abstract idealization of woman: the countless and endless variations on the *Romance of the Rose* of Jean de Meung, found in the literature of every West European language, popularized a much lower image of the feminine sex.

Parallel to the fictional works, there appeared some much more realistic and dramatic pieces directly related to sex, representing the materialistic and hedonistic aspect of the love controversy. Such writers as Chaucer and Villon — Shakespeare also in his cruder moments — express the earthy drama of the sexual relationship in real life. Shakespeare again — for there seems to be nothing he did not touch upon without success — often happily strikes a harmonious note of genuine human passion; and so do the French, with Ronsard, Remy Belleau, Louise Labé and many others.

With the decadence of classical theology and philosophy induced by the lesser Scholastics, the gap between ascetics and hedonists became even wider. This, in turn, led to the Renaissance: the rebirth of free sensuality and pagan love, as expressed by the "naughty" stories of Boccaccio and Rabelais. Such tales, which might have been delightful for Romans and Greeks who knew no better, appear to us at first sight as painful efforts to be funny through lack of respect for the sacred: in the meantime the Gospels of Christ had elevated the whole man, so that his body, the temple of the Holy Spirit, could no longer be the target of naturalistic jokes.

On the other hand, both Boccaccio and Rabelais must be taken with a grain of salt. Their works are not essentially apologies for sensuality, seduction and adultery, but satires written in a humorous vein, reactions against excessive prudery, contemporary portraits often true to life offered in a highly moral spirit. Rabelais' writings contain more lustiness than lust; and Boccaccio clearly reveals his purpose in the introduction to the Fourth Day of the *Decameron:*

Will they tear, will they lacerate me with their censures, if I, whose body heaven fashioned all apt for love, whose soul from very boyhood was dedicate to you, am not insensible to the power of the light of your eyes, to the sweetness of your honeyed words, to the flame that is kindled by your gentle sighs, but am fond

of you and sedulous to pleasure you . . . ? . . . Of a truth,
whoso taxes me thus must be one that, feeling, knowing nought
of the pleasure and power of natural affection, loves you not,
nor craves your love; and such an one I hold in light esteem.[2]

This may be taken as a reaction against the exaggerated
unearthiness of angelism, and as a valid statement of the truth
that no spiritual love is possible as long as nature is held in
contempt.

The straitjacket of Jansenism, Calvinism and Puritanism was
soon to do away with such frivolity. Burdened with a man-
made load of guilt and shame, lovemaking became secret and
repressed, a furtive and somewhat repulsive act to be performed in the dark of night with much trembling and anxiety.
The style of dress throughout Europe and America exactly
followed suit, passing from the exuberance and flamboyance
of the Renaissance to utter restraint and severity: men wore
long black coats and jackets, while women concealed whatever
charms they had received from nature by bagging them in
long-sleeved Mother Hubbards with flattened breast and chok-
ing neckline. Life, in such an attire, would necessarily have a
color of perdition and gloom.
Most of the Latin countries, however, escaped this dreadful
plight, with the exception, perhaps, of Spain — but even there
the constraint was more in the expression and clothing of the
dueña than in the hearts of the lovers. Italy seems to have
remained particularly free from the disease of gloom, for
l'amore remained at all times the favorite entertainment of
that sunny land. France and most of Western Europe suffered
under Calvinism and Jansenism, both of which, despairing of
grace and free will, cast over nature a thick veil of inhibition
and fear. The influence of Jansenius, Bishop of Ypres in

[2] J. M. Rigg translation (London: the Navarre Society, n.d.), vol. I, pp.
261-262.

Flanders, spread in the direction of Paris, leaving the Catholic Flemish themselves free to enjoy the lushness of life. This may be seen in its early and popular form in the paintings of Breughel the Elder, Teniers and Jordaens, and, in a more sophisticated manner, in those of Rubens and his followers.

It may be worth looking for a moment at the great figure of Peter Paul Rubens as an example of life both ample and virtuous. Considered by some critics the greatest painter of all time, Rubens was also an international figure entrusted with important diplomatic missions. An early portrait (in the Munich Pinacotheca) he made of himself with his first wife, Isabella Brandt, is a sober and tender scene of a happy man and woman seated hand in hand with the grace and simplicity of true love. After the death of his first wife, Rubens married Hélène Fourment, whose abundant charms adorn almost every museum of Europe and America. She is shown either as herself or as one of the countless nymphs or symbolical figures surrounding the heroes and the gods. The painter of all this glory was a man who had the world at his feet and led a princely life in his Antwerp palace, now a national museum. Yet, he managed to combine his religious fervor and his love for life in a manner that always remained above reproach, thus realizing a rare synthesis of spiritual and material values.

At the exact opposite of this optimistic and lavish state of mind, we find Puritanism — which started out as a return to the purity and simplicity of the Gospels, but ended in the unholy union of narrow-mindedness and self-righteousness. There is no doubt about the original goodwill and honesty of both Pilgrims and Puritans, nor about the liveliness of some of their numbers, even in matters of sex, as may be gathered from private memoirs of the time. The fact remains, however, that the burden of a generally negative and rigid attitude is still weighing heavily on the minds and bodies of those who claim to be their followers — a burden which may be felt on any Sunday afternoon in those American states and Canadian provinces where the Blue Laws still prevail.

Were it not for the long-lasting effects of Calvinism, Jansenism and Puritanism and their perpetuation of Manichean concepts, there would have been no need for a book such as this.

With these negative philosophies, physical love had gone underground as a wicked thing, a thing good for whores and libertines. This, in turn, brought about the inevitable reaction: with the Encyclopaedists of the Age of Enlightenment, natural love reclaimed its rights. In the eighteenth century, with the return of pagan love, pagan or classical styles in dress, furnishing and architecture were again in vogue. Love in all its romantic trappings flooded Europe as a new religion: a love which, in spite of an abundant literary expression, never amounted to much more than the naturalistic hedonism and guilt complexes of Jean-Jacques Rousseau's *Confessions*, the sterile passion and remorse of Benjamin de Constant's *Adolphe*, or the cold contempt of Jonathan Swift and of the fourth Earl of Chesterfield.

This was too much for the middle-class bourgeois spirit, which so often establishes itself as the supreme and infallible judge in matters of morals. And so, we have again, in the mid-nineteenth century, a period of rigid social codes, somber clothing, a sea of black umbrellas — and blushing hypocrisy in matters of natural love. Even piano legs received their "pantalettes." A hush-hush atmosphere prevailed, covering everything sexual with a pall of shame, so much so that it seems no true lady could have anything to do with it. How the Victorian gentlefolk ever managed to multiply will remain a physiological mystery — that is, if we take their official literature at face value, and overlook the accounts of an abundant crop of rogues.

It seems, indeed, that in spite of external differences in official style between alternating historical periods, the proportion of prudes and libertines remains almost constant. Human society consists of a number of timorous souls, a profusion of the quietly virtuous, a shifting mass of the insecure and unbalanced — and a quota of outright scoundrels who receive much more attention and publicity than they deserve.

And so, the pendulum swings, from pagan license to Scholastic prudery, from Renaissance lushness to puritanical strangulation, from Romantic freedom to Victorian hypocrisy — which of course led to the late-nineteenth century exaltation of illegitimate love, with Baudelaire and Balzac, Maupassant and Zola, and their Anglo-Saxon counterparts, of whom Charles Algernon Swinburne is perhaps the most representative. The infantile reasoning of these men seems to have been: "Love is wicked, because everybody says so; but it is also wonderful, so let us be wicked to enjoy it in full." Much of the blame falls on the shoulders of the narrow-minded Catholics of the period — including Coventry Patmore, whose domestic angelism completely lacks the cosmic fire of passion.

The spiritual revival originated at the dawn of the twentieth century seems to promise at last a stable synthesis of the human complex. In France, such men as Jacques Rivière, Léon Bloy, Ernest Psichari, Paul Claudel and the whole Neo-Scholastic school under the leadership of Jacques Maritain, finally attained a sound balance between matter and spirit, both working together in man for the glory of God. The entire work of Claudel is a hymn to love, both human and divine, and though he exalts human love to its lyrical heights, he yet clearly demonstrates its total insufficiency in regard to the allness of God. No longer do we have a scornful spirit looking down upon material things, nor a lustful animal seeking its final end in pleasure, but intelligent and sensual man living the fullness of human life, with complete respect for all that God created, and constant awareness of the primacy of the spirit.

In England, Belloc and Chesterton originated the same loud and positive creed. Yet, they did not quite reach the same note of poetry and elevation.

And what of now? There is hope, to be sure, but it is far in the background, applying to an age still to come. In spite of the spiritual revival of some, sexual love is generally either ignored or abused, exalted or degraded, deified or dragged in the mire. It shrieks on the neon signs of the theaters only to die in a divorce court. Young people rush headlong into impossible marriages without forethought or understanding, without care or concern, seeing in marriage only a means of immediate and unrestrained gratification and rejecting every notion of service and sacrifice. Public figures divorce and re-divorce, always expecting to find the perfect mate, always disappointed because all they find in the latest partner is a self-centered intemperance so perfectly matching their own that they are repelled as though they were identically charged electric poles. And so, they never find their peace.

In contemporary literature, all the old heresies and vices are offered under some gaudy jacket that presents them as great new freedoms of body and mind. Movies are being advertised precisely because of their immorality: "It's sinful: you'll love it!" The old fallacy of the absolute right to love is constantly repeated, as if it were a particular form of heroism to upset every rule of decency in order to find that unique pleasure which is to procure eternal and absolute bliss! Besides such "idealism," there is a literature of greater realism and quality, but it is one of vacuum and despair.

As with all human passions, so it is with love: in the deep and fundamental recesses of the soul there is constant hungering for the absolute, for the perfect sum of all good things. But what strange roads this hunger follows and what strange objects it pursues when it is not a true yearning for the Spirit of Love! Creatures cannot suffice to fill our desires, and yet we cannot find God by prescinding from them, for we are neither angels nor beasts, but a striving complex of body and spirit — of spiritualized matter, rather, and materialized spirit — seeking the Beatific Vision along every road of our pilgrimage on earth. It is only in the light of our final destiny that anything makes sense, and that all good things, sex included, may be taken and enjoyed as they are offered by God: with love.

II

Two Erroneous Approaches

"I'd rather learn from one bird how to sing
Than teach ten thousand stars how not to dance."

E. E. CUMMINGS

Throughout the history of human sexuality, the cyclic pattern is clear, each successive phase corresponding to the prevalence of either the Gothic or the hedonistic tendencies. These tendencies bear an important load of responsibility for the moral disorder of our present society.

The Gothic approach is the unfortunate result of unrealistic angelism, which led to a negative attitude toward the body in general and sex in particular. We will have occasion to return to it in detail. Its present expression was frozen in the form of absolute pronouncements by Scholastic philosophers some seven hundred years ago. These same pronouncements are still accepted as the truth in many a conservative institution of learning. Their proponents, generally impelled by goodwill and spiritual concern, are the unconscious victims of a narrow-minded tradition which, as we shall see, is not really that of the Church. Their world is confined to stern imperatives and legalistic duties; they see the height of sanctity in a form of asceticism that refuses pleasure because it is agreeable, and expresses itself in hell-preaching, fear of the senses, and a gen-

eral feeling of impending doom. Even the fact that they were
born of sex seems offensive to them, and they would unhesi-
tatingly attribute greater holiness to the least of the virgins
than to their own mothers. Lively and vital men and women
cannot accept their theology, which wraps the lusty and the
lustful in a single hell-bent package.

Those who continue to claim that all is well with the conservative norms are often arguing in perfect good faith that
these same norms do not impose an intolerable burden upon
them. It would, however, be most enlightening to note their
vital statistics: most of them seem to be beyond the canonical
age, or perfectly cold and inexperienced in the art of love, or
again so thoroughly brainwashed and afraid of the game of life
that they are unqualified as judges in the case. Those married
couples who, with admirable fortitude, continue to follow the
way of rigidity and declare themselves fully satisfied, cannot
be quoted in favor of the system, for what may be sufficient
for them is deadly starvation for the initiated.

It is with the latter that I am concerned here: those who,
without impairment to their moral worth or spiritual merit, are
vitally and eagerly involved in the man/woman relationship,
and see in the lack of it a crippling impoverishment. There are
many men and women who simply cannot be themselves, fully
developed and active contributors to temporal society and to
the communion of saints, unless their sexual needs are satisfied
with a reasonable measure of abundance on the three levels of
spirit, emotion and sensuality.

The worldly approach of hedonistic materialism is super-
ficially more attractive and vastly easier to follow, seeking as it
does a contact with reality unhampered by any restraint. It
considers personal pleasure as the final goal of life, and corresponds to an attitude expressed recently in the headline of a
teen-age magazine: "Nobody waits any more."

These two philosophies, that of fear and that of pleasure,
feed on each other in the maddening irrationality of a vicious

circle. The sanctimonious become more rigid as a reaction against sexual license, while the sensualists become more daring as a reaction against moralizing constraint. Both groups, sincerely convinced that their opponents are wrong, tend to justify their own excesses by quoting those of their adversaries. Since there are faults on either side — and few men can see the beam in their own eye — the reasoning assumes an appearance of validity and leads to the constant development of extremist doctrines. Both the sanctimonious and the licentious are clearly wrong.

There seems to be little reason to condemn once more the principles of materialistic hedonism: it has been done often and well. Let us rather wait for its unmasking in the light of the Virtue of Sex. What is more important, perhaps, is to root out the Gothic spirit which hides under a disguise of godliness.

N.B. The origin of all negative views of sex may be found in Platonic and Manichean dualism.

Plato came to the conclusion that the high and excellent spirit had been imprisoned in the dark and wicked body, and that the soul constantly yearned for liberation. In the theology of the ancient Persian religion of Manes, two gods of equal power, the Principle of Good and the Principle of Evil, waged a constant battle against each other. This brought about the upheavals of nature and history — and also the inner conflicts in the souls of men. Every action or phenomenon was then attributed either to Good or to Evil. In this process of division, the spiritual soul was always seen as good and the material body as evil. With such a philosophy, it was only logical to conclude that the sexual act, the very cause of the imprisonment of souls within bodies, had to be related in some way to absolute evil.

The separation of love into opposite parts — the holy relationship in the spirit and the unholy consummation in the flesh — led to many literary masterpieces that are also documents in frustration. Platonic love has a quality of unnatural longing, the main result of which is a most natural fiasco for, when the object of love is elevated to the sublimely unreal, any consummation is a letdown unworthy of a knight in shining armor.

The Church fought the Manicheans for centuries — with vigor and efficacy on the doctrinal level, but with much less conviction and success on the level of actual human life. Its theologians endorsed in part Plato's excessive spiritualism, often proposing dematerialization as an ideal and scorning the body. In much of their teaching, the body/spirit dualism led to the notion that, since sex is purely of the flesh (a point which will be discussed later), reason should reduce the physiological and emotional aspects of love to the absolute minimum required for procreation — the ideal being their complete elimination.

The truth is as remote from this distorted view as it is from materialistic hedonism. If on the one hand hedonism implies a complete misunderstanding of relative values, total disregard for human destiny and unconcern for interpersonal communication, the Gothic approach, founded on pride, implies total ignorance of one of God's greatest gifts — and total lack of simplicity and gratitude. It is fundamentally dishonest since it attempts to do away with the obvious facts of life, surviving as it does in a world that is thought to be pure but is in fact unreal. It is in a sense a living lie, or rather a lie that procures death instead of life. Since holy men cannot explain their feeling of guilt before the glories of nature by blaming its Author, they accuse the pleasure it procures. Even spiritual joys are often looked upon with disfavor.

The Gospel, the Glad Tidings, the Joyful News take on for these "holy men" the appearance of a message of gloom; perfection becomes associated with negative notions — mortification, renouncement, resignation, penance, fast, virginity — so much so that these secondary virtues or acts are equated with the highest life, often at the expense of brotherly kindness. When the Gospel idea of the freedom of the children of God within the boundaries of love gives way to scruple, fear and constraint; when the model presented for imitation is a "pale

Galilean" weakly wandering in long, flowing robes or a sugary, unwomanly Virgin ("How can she be my mother?" asked one seminarian with healthy realism. "She has no breasts!"); then no wonder modern man and woman turn away with a mixture of sadness and disgust. The challenge which is Christ is worthy of the strongest man, and that which is Mary, of the most feminine woman. Why, then, the conflict between the conservative principles of moral duty and the reality of true men and women? Because of a wrong attitude toward sex. Let us now study the written sources of so sad a misunderstanding.

ॐ III

Negative Sources

"For Godsake hold your tongue,
and let me love!" JOHN DONNE

Those who hold disparaging views on sex and marriage attempt
to support their positions by quoting the Gospels of Christ and
the Epistles of St. Paul.

"If you would be perfect . . . come, follow me." This they
interpret as meaning that the imitation of Christ's virginity
is an absolute condition to perfection. Christ, however, did
not mean that all men were to imitate him in everything he
did, but that all, whatever their station in life, were to live
as he did in the spirit of perfect love. The greatest command
of the New Testament is not one of rigorous ascetical continence, but one of generous self-giving. Its means of expression are determined by each man's and each woman's personal
calling. Since marriage is as true a vocation as any other, and
its specific expression of self-giving is the sexual union of man
and wife, this union is truly meritorious, even in its sensual
pleasure, for there is much more to sexual love than meets the
theological eye.

The pessimists frequently quote St. Paul: "The unmarried
man is anxious about the affairs of the Lord . . . but the married man is anxious about worldly affairs . . ." (I Cor. 7:32).
". . . he who marries his betrothed does well; and he who

31

refrains from marriage will do better" (I Cor. 7:38). "It is well
for a man not to touch a woman" (I Cor. 7:1). There are
several other passages with a similar teaching, but the First
Epistle to the Corinthians seems characteristic.

For these writings to be understood in their true light, they
must be placed in their historical context. St. Paul sincerely
believed that the end of the world and the day of judgment
were at hand. His counsels must be read in relation to this
imminence and urgency. If, indeed, the judgment day is almost
upon us, there is no time for marriage, but only for immediate
preparation for this tremendous event. What is the use of seeking a husband or wife, or of having children, or, in fact, of
engaging in any activity extending into a distant future, when
all is expected to come to a standstill in a very short while?
St. Paul's counsels are addressed, so to speak, to a generation
doomed to almost immediate destruction.[1] The world since
then has lasted another two thousand years and shows no sign
of proximate disintegration in spite of threats of H-bomb extinc-
tion. Hence the morality of sex and marriage are to be sought,
not with an immediate catastrophe in view as in the days of
St. Paul, but in the perspective of a continuing and self-
perfecting humanity as seen by Teilhard de Chardin.

Early interpreters of St. Paul took his advice quite literally.
When Pope Leo XIII, in his Encyclical *Arcanum divinae sapientiae,* declared formally: "It is a reproach to some of the ancients
that they showed themselves the enemies of marriage in many
ways," he had in mind, undoubtedly, the works of some of
these men who had darkened St. Paul's counsels of abstention
with a strong suspicion that the sexual act had been so thoroughly vitiated by original sin that its performance was intrinsically evil, and its pleasure doubly so.

Many of the works of St. Jerome are characteristic of this

---

[1] Cf. Craig, Clarence Tucker, Exegesis of I Corinthians, in *The Inter-
preter's Bible* (New York: Abingdon-Cokesbury Press, 1953), vol. 10,
p. 76.

state of mind, and the following text gives a clue as to its origin: "I exalt virginity to heaven, not because it is mine, but because I more greatly admire what I do not have. Preaching to others a quality lacking in oneself — this indeed amounts to a frank and embarrassing confession. If I am held down to earth by the weight of my body, is this reason enough not to admire the flight of birds?"[2]

Of all the Fathers of the Church, Jerome is perhaps the one who treated woman and sex with the greatest bitterness. Further than being a clear example of Manichean dualism, his reaction is also obviously that of a guilty conscience attempting to destroy what it could neither overcome nor integrate. It should emphatically *not* be taken as the position of the Church — and even less as that of Christ. Yet, with medieval confidence in every word written by a religious authority, the opinion of Jerome and that of another "sinner," Augustine, have been accepted for centuries as a basis for the rules of moral perfection.

In the writings of holy men, who should have known better, there are countless examples of horrified judgment: "In matrimony the act of bringing forth children is conceded, but such delights as are taken from the embrace of prostitutes are forbidden to a wife."[3] Human nature being what it is, no better encouragement could have been found for the houses of pleasure.

Again, we are told very seriously that "every over-ardent lover commits adultery with his wife."[4] Such severe pronouncements as this and the preceding one may be remotely true provided it is clearly understood that they condemn, not sexual pleasure as such, but the treating of a wife as an instrument for the satisfaction of lust. Yet, they are most damaging to

[2] St. Jerome, *Comm. sup. epist. ad Eph.*, 5:27.
[3] St. Jerome, *Adv. Jovim.*, lib. 1, n. 49.
[4] Sextus Pithagoricus, *Sententioli* (Bibliotheca veterum patrum, de la Bigne), vol. 5, n. 222.

marriage, since they seem to cover also the perfectly legitimate pursuit of erotic harmony within the sacramental state of matrimony.

It would be only too easy to quote hundreds of examples in the same tone by such authorities as St. Basil, St. John Chrysostom, St. Gregory, and almost every other saint of the period. How could such great and reasonable men propound such negative and narrow principles? The explanation may be found in the historical circumstances of their writings and in the purpose they sought to achieve. As indicated in the historical sketch above, these early Fathers lived during the period of decay of the Greco-Roman culture, at a time of wholesale sexual corruption. In the midst of the worst public and private vice, and fighting its torrent, these few men had stood up in defense of moral virtue, desperately trying to defend their disciples against the waves of disorder. No wonder that, in their eagerness to protect their flock, they gathered up the cockle with the wheat, mixing the false doctrines of pessimistic dualism with true notions of purity and chastity.

This same defensive tradition survived the Dark Ages, for we find it expressed anew in the works of the Pre-Scholastics, Bede, Anselm, and Bernard of Clairvaux in his early works. The influential author of the *Libri sententiarum,* Peter Lombard, strongly supports it once more. All this could be confirmed with scholarly quotations, but why add such unnecessary weight to our book?

Instead of elaborating a more encouraging and objective doctrine, the great Scholastics themselves relied entirely on the now semi-officially established negative tradition. Instead of looking with open eyes at life as it actually is, they were content to echo the Fathers' thunderings and to establish their theology of marriage on the same narrow foundation as had their predecessors. In fact, the Scholastics unquestioningly accepted as authorities on sex those very men whose main concern had been to extinguish its fire. And so, we find in Scholastic writings a perfect sequence to the ancient pessimism: "In the act of human generation, there is always present vicious corruption, almost always immoderate pleasure, and often also dishonest intention. . . . In the act of generation there is major shame." This is from the pen of a good and holy man, St. Bonaventure.[5]

Even the great Thomas Aquinas is not above reproach in this matter, for, after having declared that "if we suppose corporeal nature to have been created by the good God, we cannot hold that those things which pertain to the conservation of that nature and for which nature has a propensity are entirely evil," [6] he goes on to say: "The shamefulness of concupiscence which always accompanies the marriage act is a shamefulness, not of guilt, but of penalty." [7] Thus, he asserts that intercourse is never free from shame.

Again, he writes: "There was marriage in paradise, but no carnal intercourse." — "Marriage is permitted in the state of infirmity by indulgence." — "The turpitude that always accompanies the marriage act and always causes shame is a turpitude of punishment, not of sin, for man is naturally ashamed of any defect." [8]

Let us note in passing that a theologian, even when he happens to be a saint and a Doctor of the Church, is not necessarily infallible in all he writes. In fact, it would take volumes to record the imperfections and inadequacies of men elevated to the highest honors of canonization and scholarly applause. This should not decrease our respect for them but, on the contrary, encourage us to seek true sanctity and wisdom in spite of our own failures.

In order to avoid any misunderstanding, I wish to emphasize that there are many good priests who provide an abundance of sound counseling in matters of sex and marriage. My point

[5] *Opera Omnia* (Quaracchi, 1882-1902), vol. III, p. 755a.
[6] *Summa Theologica*, p. III, q. 41, a. 3 (London: Burns & Oates, 1932), vol. XIX, p. 82.
[7] Ibid., ad. 3, p. 83.
[8] Ibid., q. 42, a. 4, pp. 93-94; q. 49, a. 1, p. 144; a. 4, ad. 4, p. 154.

is that they have reached this level of wisdom, not by means of traditional seminary teachings and manuals, but in spite of them. It is perfectly safe and easy to follow the book, avoiding personal involvement, original thought, and individual responsibility, and to judge all problems of marriage from the viewpoint of a legalistic and infallible high court applying the letter of the law. On the contrary, it takes much courage and intelligence to admit and profess that the law contains many remnants of medieval superstition, in spite of *nihil obstat, imprimatur* and *imprimi potest*.

For the clerical mind to reach such a point of wisdom, a personal conversion is needed, a natural conversion away from the unnatural rigidity of theoretical notions. Through efforts of their own, some religious counselors have been able to break away from the conservative routine, to reach a positive, dynamic view of life, revealed in a charity that is no longer paternalistic condescension, but a true understanding of married tenderness in its sexual aspects. They no longer consider sex as an enemy of perfection, but see it as a wonderful gift they have willfully foregone, but which they encourage and admire and are happy to see flourishing in others. They are capable of independent judgment and are willing to face reality as it is instead of accepting blindly what it is said to be. But this effort of readjustment and rethinking is not made often enough, nor does it seem to be encouraged by superiors. That is why the layman has to speak, hoping to be the voice of the more enlightened clergy which obedience forces to be still.

It is strange to note the strength of the negative prejudice against sex and marriage which made the Scholastics endorse unqualifiedly so many teachings that were obviously exaggerated in their rigidity. Such men as Thomas Aquinas and Bonaventure were much more perspicacious in other matters. When they happened to come across what they felt to be errors in the writings of the *authentici* — those authorities whose reliability had been established by universal tradition —

they never accused them openly of having made mistakes, but produced so-called "pious" interpretations which gently forced the sense back into line. In all matters of sex, however, their piety took the form of unquestioning endorsement.

In the monumental edition of the *Works of St. Bonaventure,* the Franciscan editors offer an illuminating note: "It seems that such [negative] teachings are consistent with the doctrines of the Fathers — doctrines which are somewhat more severe than those currently taught." [9] This in turn is a pious way of saying that they are completely wrong, even in the eyes of conservative theologians of the turn of the century. Unfortunately, however, such cramped notions became imbedded in the minds of a number of moralists who accepted them as part of the true Christian tradition, and handed them down to our present age. For the negative attitude is not a mere sin of the past: it may be found in full vigor in almost every formal treatise on the ethics of marriage, and even in some contemporary studies on the theology of sex.

Before we pass to more encouraging views, let us consider two instances of clerical rigorism that deserve to be noted.

The following passage is an actual translation from the *Compendium Theologiae Asceticae* by Adolphus a Denderwindeke, O.F.M., Cap., a manual of ascetical theology published in 1921 with full imprimatur:

> The sense of touch, given especially by God to man for the preservation of the human species, is not, like the other senses, located in any one part of the body, but extends throughout the whole. Hence its custody is supremely necessary. This sense is vile and animal: everywhere throwing poisoned food before the will, it lies in ambush in every limb: it seeks delights that are supremely pestiferous and more deadly than any other, that is, the sensual and the impure, which take life away from the soul and lead it to eternal exile. (p. 119)

[9] IV, Sent., d. 31, a. 2, q. 1, scholion, *Opera Omnia,* vol. IV, p. 718.

The first thing worthy of note is that the author is so obsessed with sex that he sees no other use for the sense of touch than the performance of acts of sensuous impurity. There is also here a flagrant contradiction that amounts to a heresy, and which neither author nor censor seems to have noticed: the sense of touch is made by God, and yet it is said to be absolutely vile and animal.

A current English translation, released from Rome, of one of the Papal documents on marriage contains the following paragraph:

> To exalt, therefore, as is frequently done today, the generative function in even its right and moral form of conjugal life, is not only an error and an aberration. Doing this brings also with it the danger of the deviation of the mind and affections which hinder and suffocate good and lofty sentiments, especially among young people still without experience and ignorant of the snares of life.[10]

Since a goodly share of the present work was to consist in exaltation, if not precisely of the generative function, at least of the complete sexual relationship, this text came as a severe blow. But the tone of it sounded wrong. A comparison with the original Italian of the *Acta Apostolicae Sedis* soon revealed that two words had been dropped in the translation, two little words that made all the difference: *oltre misura*. What the Pope had written was this: "To exalt, therefore, *beyond measure*, as is frequently done . . . ," which is quite another story. But some translator in his misplaced zeal — for in such important matters I cannot believe in mere oversight — distorted the text in order to increase its severity!

Only after the final judgment will rash and incompetent theologians realize the immensity of sufferings and losses to the Church their errors and vacillations, enforced by authority,

[10] *Moral Questions Affecting Married Life—the Apostolate of the Midwife* (New York: Paulist Press, 1951), p. 21, n. 560.

imposed unnecessarily upon the faithful. "They bind heavy burdens, hard to bear, and lay them on men's shoulders . . ." (Matthew 23:4). By contrast, immense goodwill and humility may be seen in the obedience of so many lay people who would be justified in asking embarrassing questions, but are content to suffer in silence. Now that the discussion has been forced out into the open, theologians must speak the language of civilized man, account for their every word and judgment, and put their personal signatures to the opinions they express instead of hiding behind the façade of an institution, be it ever so highly placed. And this is doubly true of matters of so vital import as those of sex and marriage.[11]

The negative examples quoted above are far from representing the universal opinion of the Church. For a sounder view, let us now take a look at the positive writings on human love.

[11] The negative attitude toward sex and woman is not confined to religious writers. Schopenhauer and Tolstoy were dreadful pessimists, as Dr. Karl Stern demonstrates in *The Flight from Woman* (New York: Farrar, Strauss & Giroux, 1965). Then there is also the most ungallant of Frenchmen, Montherlant.

IV

Positive Sources

> "There will arise tomorrow, perhaps, a new type of
> sanctity, in which love of God will be completely
> human."   GUSTAVE THIBON

" 'This at last is bone of my bones and flesh of my flesh; she shall
be called Woman . . .' " (Gen. 2:23). How long had Adam possessed the earth and everything on it, possessed them alone and
wonderingly, seeking what had not yet been made? We do not
know. The biblical words express admirably the feelings of a
young man yearning for the love and companionship of a wife,
and finally discovering her with a shout of joy, for indeed, "it is
not good for man to live alone."

In the biblical expression of the beginning of human love,
there is a tragic dualism: a great gift of God tainted by sin,
a shout of joy and a cry of shame, immense delight cut short
by suffering and death. Gift, joy and delight are from God;
sin, shame and death, from man. This same dualism is present
in the love life of every couple, and it will be so until the end
of mankind and the completion of the number of the elect. But
a promise of salvation was made to Abraham, and even before
it came to pass, marriage was flowering on earth, as witnessed
by the many instances of conjugal love remembered in the
Old Testament.

Then, of course, there is the Song of Songs, perhaps the

greatest love poem ever composed, and certainly the most often printed. So much has been written about its interpretation that we are almost unable to read it objectively. Layer after layer of symbolism encrusts our memory, disguising perhaps the simple truth. It is part of the Canon of the Bible, and therefore classified officially as an inspired work. It is quite obviously a poem of love, but of what love does it sing? Is it primarily the conversation of God with the soul, of Christ with his Church, or of a very human lover with his very earthly beloved?

Whatever the final interpretation, one thing is certain: as is the case with most prophets, the inspired author had no clear foresight of the full and far-reaching effects of his words. While commentators may be justified in seeking to determine every possible meaning, they must always remember that in the writer's mind the words must have had a clear literal sense that has as much right to sacred endorsement as the more hidden symbolism. The Song of Songs, then, may be read as an expression of true human love fully approved by God.

It is delightfully frank and enthusiastic. The fullness of sensual delight reaches us even through the cautious wording of translations. It cannot be disguised even in the severe Latin of Jerome's Vulgate. The English scholars responsible for the King James Version happily render the physical and emotional pleasure of the marital relationship:

> Thou hast ravished my heart, my sister, my spouse; thou hast ravished my heart with one of thine eyes, with one chain of thy neck.
> How fair is thy love, my sister, my spouse! how much better is thy love than wine! and the smell of thine ointments than all spices!
> Thy lips, O my spouse, drop as the honeycomb: honey and milk are under thy tongue; and the smell of thy garments is like the smell of Lebanon.
> A garden inclosed is my sister, my spouse; a spring shut up, a fountain sealed (4:9-12).
> How fair and how pleasant art thou, O love, for delights!

This thy stature is like to a palm tree, and thy breasts to clusters of grapes.

I said, I will go up to the palm tree, I will take hold of the boughs thereof: now also thy breasts shall be as clusters of the vine, and the smell of thy nose like apples;

And the roof of thy mouth like the best wine for my beloved, that goeth down sweetly, causing the lips of those that are asleep to speak.

I am my beloved's, and his desire is toward me (7:6-10).

Passing to the New Testament, we find several most encouraging texts on marriage. Christ's presence with his mother at the celebration of the wedding in Cana may be seen not only as a formal endorsement of the ceremony itself, but also as an approval of it as a joyful family feast. Christ even goes so far as to provide the wine to make the occasion more festive.

Then there is the solemn confirmation of the sacred and divine character of marriage:

. . . Have you not read that he who made them from the beginning made them male and female, and said: "For this reason man shall leave his father and mother and be joined to his wife, and the two shall become one"? So they are no longer two, but one. What therefore God has joined together, let no man put asunder (Mt. 19:4-6).

As for St. Paul, in spite of his apparently negative views explained above, he gave us several declarations and counsels showing his great respect for the married state:

So I would have younger widows marry, bear children, rule their households, and give the enemy no occasion to revile us (1 Tm. 5:14).

Husbands, love your wives, as Christ loved the Church and gave himself up for her, that he might sanctify her. . . . Even so husbands should love their wives as their own bodies.

He who loves his wife loves himself. For no man ever hates his own flesh, but nourishes and cherishes it, as Christ does the church, because we are members of his body. "For this reason a man shall leave his father and mother and be joined to his wife, and the two shall become one." This is a great mystery, and I mean in reference to Christ and the church; however, let each one of you love his wife himself, and let the wife see that she respect her husband (Eph. 5:25-33).

There are many other encouraging passages.

By contrast, positive notes on marriage in the writings of the early Fathers are disappointingly rare. Yet the picture is not entirely bleak. Cyril of Alexandria, for instance, has some good words to say of the marriage at Cana.

Since the wedding is celebrated chastely and honorably, the Mother of the Savior is there; and he himself invited along with the disciples, comes not so much to dine as to perform a miracle — and also to sanctify the source of man's bodily genera- tion. For it was fitting that he who was to renew the very nature of man and recall the whole of it to a better state, should not only impart a blessing on those who had already been born, but also that he should prepare grace for those to be born in later times, by making their birth holy. Honorable marriage is made sacred and the curse against woman removed: no longer will they bear children in sorrow, now that Christ has blessed the very starting point of our generation.

Clement of Alexandria also, in his *Stromata,* comes strongly to the defense of the matrimonial state, answering an attack by the Gnostics.

In the Pre-Scholastic period, many voices are raised in doubt concerning the prevalent negative teachings on sex, among them that of Abelard: "In forcing us to admit that sexual pleasure itself is a sin, it seems that they rely on authority rather than on logical proofs." [1]

---

[1] *Ethica,* c. 3, PL 178, 640.

As for the Scholastics themselves, their views are not consistently negative in spite of the general trend. Both Alexander of Hales and Duns Scotus recognized the intrinsic goodness of the sexual act at a time when a majority of theologians were teaching that "excusing goods" were needed to make up for its intrinsic shamefulness. There are, however, many nuances in the description of the required "goods." Thomas Aquinas, who often refers to them as a condition of righteous marriage, comes close to the Scotist opinion when he is led to define their nature.

Before coming to the doctrine of modern Popes, we may quote two more authors on the positive side of the controversy.

Denis the Carthusian, a Flemish monk of the fifteenth century, wrote a whole treatise *On the Praise of Conjugal Life,* and this is one of the points he makes: "The marriage act can be an act of charity or spiritual love: for all good works are necessarily the fruit of spiritual and divine love." [2]

And Leonard Lessius (1554-1623), a Jesuit theologian, Professor at Louvain University, definitely settles the question of the presence of the Holy Spirit during sexual activity — a presence which had been sternly denied by some of his contemporaries: "It cannot but follow that the Holy Spirit is indeed present during this activity, insofar as it is an act of justice or charity or religion or some other virtue. For the will is unable to aim at such virtues without help from the Holy Spirit." [3]

These two texts provide a theological foundation for the notion expressed in the title of this book, *The Virtue of Sex.*

In the writings and speeches of recent Popes, we find many encouraging views in strong contrast with ancient pessimism.

In his Encyclical *Arcanum divinae sapientiae* of February 10, 1880, Pope Leo XIII brings forth in a beautiful paragraph the positive side of the Catholic tradition:

[2] "De laud. vit. conj.," *Works,* 38, 63.
[3] *Prael. de sac. mat.,* c. 1, dub. 2.

But what was decreed and constituted in respect to marriage by the authority of God, has been more fully and more clearly handed down to us, by tradition and the written Word, through the Apostles, those heralds of the laws of God. To the Apostles, indeed, as our masters, are to be referred the doctrines which our holy Fathers, the Councils, and the Tradition of the Universal Church have always taught, namely, that Christ our Lord raised marriage to the dignity of a sacrament; that to husband and wife, guarded and strengthened by the heavenly grace which his merit gained for them, he gave power to attain holiness in the married state; and that, in a wondrous way, making marriage an example of the mystical union between Himself and His Church. He not only perfected that love which is according to nature, but also made the natural union of one man with one woman far more perfect through the bond of heavenly love.

In the Encyclical *Casti connubii,* Pope Pius XI has this to say:

This mutual inward molding of husband and wife, this determined effort to perfect each other, can in a very real sense, as the Roman Catechism teaches, be said to be the chief reason and purpose of matrimony, provided it be looked at not in the restricted sense as instituted for the proper conception and education of the child, but more widely as the blending of life as a whole and the mutual interchange and sharing thereof.

This seems to be the first authoritative statement of the "personalistic" theory of marriage. It is immensely important in the controversy concerning the "primary" and "secondary" ends of marriage in that it shows the primary to be a matter of viewpoint, and not an absolute in the essential order.

In his speech *The Apostolate of the Midwife* addressed on October 29, 1951, to delegates attending the Congress of the Catholic Union of Midwives in Italy, Pope Pius XII declared: "The marriage contract which confers upon husband and wife the right to satisfy the inclination of nature, sets them up in a certain state of life, the married state."

It is worthy to note that the Pope carefully avoided the ancient and misleading expression "satisfaction of concupiscence" and replaced it by the much more accurate and positive term, "inclination of nature."

Again, he says: "The proper and more profound meaning of the conjugal right must consist in this, that the union of the bodies is the expression and the actuation of the personal and affectionate [affective] union."

Finally, in his comments on the use of the rhythm method, Pius XII clearly declares that so long as the intention is right and there is no obligation to have more children, the performance of the marriage act is perfectly legitimate during the period of infertility, even with the formal intention of avoiding procreation.

There should come at this point an indication of the contemporary moral theologians who fully conform with such a positive tradition and with the directives of recent Popes. There is in existence, however, not one official manual of moral theology that comes anywhere near providing an adequate teaching in matters of sex. Let me repeat: *there is no good seminary textbook on the subject.* Several instances of the imperfection of existing works have been shown above; they seem to reflect a general trend. Even the more encouraging works, such as that by Vermeersch, seem to lag far behind other books written by priests and addressed to laymen, particularly in Belgium, France and Germany. The best of these are probably *Love and Control,* by Cardinal Suenens of Malines-Brussels,[4] and a volume slim in size but great in value, Father Daniel Planque's *The Theology of Sex in Marriage,*[5] which may serve as a most useful guide to those contemplating matrimony. The notions expressed in this work are encouraging, positive and up to date:

[4] Westminster, Md.: Newman Press, 1962.
[5] Notre Dame, Ind.: Fides, 1963.

The carnal act becomes the expression, and as it were the sign, at the physical level, of the fusion of the most spiritual and most personal aspects of the husband and the wife themselves; and this whole panoply of joys of the body, of the heart, and of the soul becomes not only a blessing attached by God to the normal exercise of sexual life, but also the means of achieving in joy the perfect unity of the couple who are destined to give life (p. 42).

Viewing conjugal intimacies as being at the service of love, is not only to have a better understanding of the natural order such as God has willed it: it is also to rehabilitate the carnal act and pleasures which a too-narrow concept of the finality of marriage has helped to discredit (p. 77).

To conclude this section: I am definitely *not* saying that the Church has been wrong in matters of sex since its very earliest days and that now is the time of enlightenment. On the contrary, I have demonstrated sufficiently that there has been a constant flow of realistic, warm and true teaching, beginning in the Old Testament, confirmed in the New, and continuing in our days in the works of many open-minded theologians. The fact remains, however, that throughout almost all its history the Church has been excessively influenced by a current of pessimism and fear of sex whose followers were often louder than the advocates of truth. Because of the great number of these prophets of gloom, even in our modern world, and because of the intensity of the effort it takes to debunk them, such an effort appears to the short-sighted as an attack on Catholic morality, while in fact it is but a defense of its true spirit.

In the absence of intelligent and qualified theological solutions to the problems of sex, it is all too easy for moralists to hide behind the opinion of honorable men of the past whose doctrine could be no more complete than the fragmentary physiology and psychology of their time. The result is often abuse of authority precisely because of the lack of proper understanding.

The revival of truth will consist, not in the revision of a few extrinsic rules of conduct, nor even in a dramatic reversal of doctrine concerning contraceptives, but in the elaboration of the *true and complete* principles of sexual morality. Logical solutions to the most difficult problems will then be seen to flow naturally from the corrected premises, putting an end to the confusion, doubt and pain characteristic of the present state of affairs. The elaboration of these principles must begin by a clarification of the notion of natural law.

V

The Natural Law

"We shall find this truth formed within us, and
ourselves formed anew within it and thus becoming one with it." BLESSED JOHN RUYSBROECK

The study of the natural law touches upon the very foundation
of morality and is essential to the reconstruction of the ecclesiastic laws on sex. It deserves therefore the utmost attention and
care. We must consider in turn three distinct attitudes, the
pragmatic, the conservative and the progressive.

THE PRAGMATIC ATTITUDE

The pragmatic viewpoint is clearly expressed in a series of
articles, *Catholics and Birth Control*, published in *The New
York Times* between August 8 and 11, 1963. The author, Mr.
George Barrett, contends that the Catholic position is unsound
when it relies on the natural law, since man is constantly correcting nature and improving on it.

A misunderstanding arises from the different possible mean-
ings of the word "nature." In the physical sense, nature desig-
nates material creatures in their concrete reality, as for instance
in the expressions "a natural phenomenon" and "the laws of
nature." What is considered is the recurrent pattern of be-

49

havior of material objects as perceived and expressed by experimental science. Nature, in this sense, is phenomenal and not essential. It is constantly changing along the paths of evolution, and its course is being accelerated by human techniques. It cannot possibly serve as the basis of an unchanging moral law.

Even the argument that the very laws of evolution are themselves unchanging adds no sufficient weight to physical nature to make it serve as a foundation for ethics. A stable system of morality cannot be made to depend upon immutable rules *of evolution*, since we are participating, not in the stable rules themselves, but in the changes they bring about. The rules are in the conceptual order, the changes in that of physical reality.

Any attempt to make moral precepts depend upon physical nature, even within its limited constancy, is bound to fail because it gives excessive attention to accidental characteristics that do not essentially affect the principles of human conduct. Such things as the color of the skin, skeletal conformation, rural or urban dwelling, habits of work or recreation, travel or communication facilities do not make a man to be more or less of a man; they pertain to the sociologist, not to the moralist.

Advocates of a pragmatic and changing morality often argue from the fact that contemporary life has many facets of which the moral theologian had never even dreamed, and that the principles of morality should be altered to fit such novelties. The answer to this contention is very simple: everything man does and will ever do that has any moral implication will always consist in a free human act, to be judged in relation to the immutable essence of humanity, which is human "nature" in the second sense of the word. To drive an ox-cart or pilot a jet plane, to walk a mile or travel to the moon, to grind flour between two stones or produce new compounds by juggling molecules — these are not actions of a different order demanding a different morality, but merely elaborate variations of the free human act.

In the Christian context, "nature" refers to the unchanging *essence* of beings. When we refer to human nature, we mean

that by which man is man, that by which he is essentially different from any other species of being, that by which he will
always differ as long as he is himself. The fact that he may
have evolved from a lower form of life is irrelevant: what
counts is what he is now. The natural law, or law of human
nature, is the law, not of a passing phenomenon, but of a metaphysical entity endowed with constant and perceptible characteristics, living in a definite milieu which makes it partake both
of physical nature and of grace.

The fundamental premise of Christianity is its directional
axis: we know whence we originate, where we are going, and
why. Every free act in accord with the logic of this motion will
be good. The quality of this moral good may be perfected with
the development of civilization. Man himself is evolving, not
in his essence, but in his accidental perfectibility. What had
been tolerable in a state of lesser refinement — for instance,
bigamy and divorce under the Old Testament — becomes unacceptable and thus immoral as soon as humanity reaches the
level of a better understanding of its dignity.

THE CONSERVATIVE ATTITUDE

The conservative attitude is characterized by a variety of
misinterpretations and a number of specific errors. Among the
prevalent misinterpretations are the following:

Some moralists understand the natural law as if it were
nothing but the Decalogue, or a part of it. The Decalogue is
all well and good, but it is not enough: it belongs to the Old
Testament and expresses the law of fear, the law of commands
and prohibitions. We live now in the light of the Resurrection
of Christ, under the law of love. While all the principles of
the Decalogue remain in force, they have been raised to a
higher level of obligation. No longer do we obey out of constraint, but out of willful conformation with Providence. The
law of love covers every instance of the free human act above
and beyond what the Ten Commandments prescribe or forbid.

Others understand the natural law as being the expression
of their subjective and pessimistic view of nature. The "naturalness" of a principle rests with them on nothing more than
prejudice, reinforced by a repetitive and groundless tradition.
For such minds, nature — not "human nature" as such, but the
physical aspect of man and woman — is so closely associated
with concupiscence and sin that the right thing to do is to
have the least possible contact with it. Natural law, in their
eyes, demands that we shun sensual pleasure, that we make
love in the most furtive and discreet manner, in the dark of
night, in haste and with a measure of disgust — and only according to an accepted routine, in the "natural" position.

"Intercourse can be disorderly, that is, unnatural and improper because of the manner of lying together. . . . This
occurs for instance when the man is underneath, or approaches
from the rear as do cattle, or from the side, or while sitting
or standing, or in some other unusual way. This is contrary
to nature." [1]

Such solemn pronouncements would be delightfully funny
if they were not also immensely damaging. Not so long ago
this nonsense constituted the normal educational fare of confessors, who then, in total innocence and ignorance, proceeded
to poison the lives of countless married couples.

There is great absurdity in leaving the detailed rules of
sexual morality entirely in the hands of clerical celibates.
Experience is needed as a basis for lawmaking. Intimate contact with a naked woman is one of the necessary sources from
which to draw the norms of proper conduct, and no entirely
valid judgment of the man/woman relationship could ever be
formulated without it. I am not suggesting that every moralist
take to himself a warm and responsive wife — although the
idea may have some merit: I am only wondering why those
who do not have such experience believe themselves entitled
to impose dogmatic judgments upon others who do.

NB.

[1] *Opus theologicum morale*, edited by Dominicus Palmieri (Prati: Gia-
chetti, 1890), vol. II, p. 726.

A distinction should be made between rules that are clearly of divine origin, such as monogamy, respect for marriage, the procreative end, and others of a disciplinary nature that are determined by ecclesiastical law.

While churchmen are invested with authority in their proper field, which is that of the spirit, they lack the charisma of universal wisdom. In those matters that are clearly not of their domain, they should listen before hurling *odium theologicum* at perfectly harmless and even virtuous expressions of sexual love, as they have done so often in the past on the strength of completely false and artificial notions. They often failed because their judgments, instead of being existential, were founded on preconceived universal categories.

Sexually speaking, humanity is made up of two general groups, the initiated and the uninitiated, the latter comprising a large number of married couples. Neither group has the competence to judge or even counsel the other since it lacks experiential understanding of the other's ways. The strict and conservative have no right to scorn those who enjoy a rich sensual life — and vice versa — nor may the initiated totally disregard moral laws imposed by the uninitiated. Both groups must be brought together for a realistic solution. The moralist must reconsider very seriously certain practical aspects of ethical discipline, including birth control, not by his own traditional methods alone, but in direct consultation with the lover.

A third and more recent misconception of the natural law tends to concentrate attention on a *bodily function* considered independently of its effect on the whole human complex and on society. It is this inadequate understanding that is invoked as the definitive argument against any positive method of contraception. The idea seems to be that physical nature, as created by God, must be left to run its course unimpeded, whatever the consequences affecting man, woman or child. This is a kind of materialistic determinism that prevents reason from affecting the outcome of an act which, after all, is material on its lowest level only. Biological necessity is allowed to take precedence over personal and spiritual values — which is much more unnatural than the so-called unnaturalness of contraceptives, for it opposes, not merely physical nature, but human nature and the orderly pre-eminence of will and intelligence over matter.[2]

In conservative teachings, there are not only misinterpretations of the natural law, but also a number of major inconsistencies. A surprising divergence existed until recently between moralists concerning the duty of fecundity. A complete and scholarly study of contradictory opinions, all supported by an imprimatur, would take up too much time and space. Suffice it to say that until the publication of Pius XII's *Allocution to the Midwives*, which clearly indicated the duty of procreation, several highly esteemed moralists had doubted whether it existed at all. They understood the command "increase and multiply" as referring, not to individual couples, but to mankind in general. They may have been right in fact, but they certainly were not in accord with traditional principles, since the system of sexual morality from the Middle Ages on had rested on the notion that procreation alone justified intercourse. They were either advocating marriage without intercourse, which is absurd, or pulling the rug from under the whole conservative edifice.

There are still other inconsistencies in the system. Why the irrational fixation, the obsessive compulsion that makes the traditional majority judge matters of sex differently from any other? Why eliminate the Levitical law and yet hang on to the one sad story of Onan, which, as modern theologians will

---

[2] Father Bernard Häring has seen this very clearly: "A natural law consideration which places the accent only on a right biological performance of the conjugal act remains on the level of mere animals and considers as primary what man has in common with the animals. It forgets the higher needs of the person and therefore necessarily remains a very poor minimalism." (*Homiletic and Pastoral Review*, July, 1964).

agree, is irrelevant to the problems of our age?[3] Why accept the principle of the sovereignty of man over nature, and yet refuse to apply it to sex — where man must consent to be tortured by it? Why propose the principle of double effect, and yet frantically forbid its application to contraceptive practices?

The most asinine pretexts are sometimes adduced in support of the traditional view: "If rules were ever changed, many people would be disappointed because they would feel they had suffered in vain." Charity demands that references be omitted here, but the argument was actually published. What it amounts to is this: "Perhaps we were wrong, but let us continue to be wrong and make all married couples suffer so as not to disappoint our earlier victims!"

There are also specific errors in the conservative position. The most widespread is *clericalism.* Discussions in the Vatican Council's meetings in November 1964 vividly brought out two contrasting notions of the Church: the conservative view, that it consists in a political body established over members of an inferior rank, and the progressive, that it is constituted by the assembly of the faithful served by the priestly hierarchy. There is no doubt as to the tendency of the Council Fathers: an immense majority favors the latter view, although the final draft of *De Ecclesia* seems to be a compromise.

Many of the clerically minded see in marriage some inferiority "by nature," since they tend to see the perfection of the Church of God in a hierarchy of celibates invested with ecclesiastical authority. Hence, the theory of the "state of perfection," which will be discussed in Chapter VI.

Again, the conservative position suffers from a taint of *false spiritualism* — a distortion of the natural law which tends to consider ideal man as a pure spirit, to insist on the absolute dominion of reason over will and love, to see the perfect life as a constant and unconditional rejection of the body. This is

[3] "The use of the biblical argument (Gen. 38:9f) in *Casti Connubii* does not prove what it wished to prove." Bernard Häring, loc. cit.

frequently combined with an arrogant affirmation of the superiority of the male (the rational principle) over the female
(the affective principle), so that ideal humanity is represented
by the scornful and disincarnate male completely disassociated
from his natural partner, woman, and from everything that ties
him to the material creation. Such an attitude is opposed not
only to the natural law, as reason sees it, but also to the supernatural fact of the Incarnation. This will be covered in
Chapter VII.

Once more, the conservative position suffers from an excessively *penitential* slant. One of the reasons why the clerical
approach to marriage is so often negative is that all matters
de sexto et nono are taught from the viewpoint of the confessor.
Sexual activities are considered, not in their potential perfection, but in their possible defects. The confessor's part is not
to reward the virtuous, but to convey the mercy of Christ to
the sinner. Because of the confessor's training, he is often so
deeply concerned with the possibility of grievous sin that he
may become blind to anything else. Even in treatises whose
purpose is not primarily penitential, in manuals of moral theology, for instance, the priest has become accustomed to finding marriage treated in its legalistic requirements as a contract,
in its sinfulness under the capital sin of lust, and in its control
under the negative virtues of continence or temperance. In
the parts dealing with its sacramentality, marriage is seen from
the viewpoint of impediments in an atmosphere of impending
catastrophe. The enriching effects of matrimonial grace are
entirely overlooked while the notion of sexual sin is grossly
overstressed. This is discussed in Chapter VIII.

Finally, there is in the conservative approach extreme *unreality*. The Latin Church, from the Scholastics on, has lived in
an atmosphere of abstract dogmatism or definitionism — the
unhealthy habit of denying mystery, of attempting to define
the undefinable and to reduce it to absolute categories. This
produces great clarity in the mind — a clarity related to an
artificially constructed universe that seems rationally sound but

seldom coincides with the world as it is. There is clarity, yes, but also dryness and inadequacy, for such an attitude does not properly face the mystery of the person: it eliminates the sense of awe, of constant wonder, and overlooks many of love's most appealing faces. It makes of the intellect the measure of God's grace, ignoring the unity of the human complex, body, heart and soul. It results in the establishment of rules of conduct that lack the strength of living contact with reality. This will be considered at length in the Chapters IX and X on birth control.

The marriage relationship cannot be summarized as a series of commands of abstract virtues and prohibitions of physiological acts, for the virtues seem unreal while the acts have an all-too-obvious appeal. The pleasure of sinning, much more immediate than the reward of abstract virtue, assumes the greater existential value. Here, even supposing the total verity of the conservative system regulating sexual morality, and without falling into "situation ethics," there still would be place for decisions corresponding to what the positive law calls "equity" — that is, corrective measures inspired by the natural law itself — in cases in which damage would result from the overstrict application of some legal statute. This proves, not that the statute is wrong, but that its formulation is not properly adapted to every possible instance of life.

Thomas Aquinas is very clear on this point. He rejects the rigid and uncompromising application of any universal principle to contingent human acts — all the more so when the principle tends to codify some specific detail of human behavior, since a greater number of conditions are then added, which in turn amount to a greater risk of inapplicability of the principle to individual instances of life.

To the Natural Law belong those things to which man is inclined naturally; and among these it is proper to man to be inclined to act according to reason. Now the process of reason is from the common to the proper, as stated in *Phys. 1*. The speculative reason, however, is differently situated in this matter, from the practical reason. For, since the speculative reason is busied chiefly with necessary things, which cannot be otherwise than they are, its proper conclusions, like the universal principles, contain the truth without fail. The practical reason, on the other hand, is busied with contingent matters, about which human actions are concerned; and consequently, although there is necessity in the general principles, the more we descend to matters of detail, the more frequently we encounter defects. Accordingly then in speculative matters truth is the same in all men, both as to principles and as to conclusions; although the truth is not known to all as regards the conclusions, but only as regards the principles which are called common notions. But in matters of action, truth or practical rectitude are not the same for all, as to matters of detail, but only as to the general principles; and where there is the same rectitude in matters of detail, it is not equally known to all.

. . . And this principle will be found to fail the more, according as we descend further into detail . . . because the greater the number of conditions added, the greater the number of ways in which the principle may fail.[4]

This opinion of the Master of Scholasticism corresponds to a much more liberal view than that of his would-be followers who tend to apply detailed statutes with a rigidity that is incompatible with their limited scope.

The principal error of the conservatives is to have injected an absolute character into relative matters. This may be demonstrated in two ways: first by analyzing the notion of intrinsic evil, and then by showing that by some mysterious process the decrees of natural law have changed in the minds of theologians from the fluidity of disciplinary commands to the rigidity of dogmatic imperatives.

First, then, let us consider intrinsic evil. *Metaphysically speaking* intrinsic evil simply does not exist, since evil-as-such is synonymous with non-being-as-such. Even the Worst, the

[4] *Summa Theologica*, Ia, IIae, a. 4, concl. (London: Burns and Oates, 1927), vol. 8, pp. 47, 48.

Evil One — personified in the Greek text of the Lord's Prayer, but reduced in the English version to impersonal "evil" — cannot possibly be Absolute or Intrinsic or Necessary Evil. He is indeed the Father of Lies, but he is also a fallen archangel who, in spite of his moral failure, retains the metaphysical splendor of his original essence. To associate intrinsic evil with necessary evil implies an inner contradiction. The attribution of necessity to evil gives it more reality than it can contain, for necessity is an attribute of being — not only that, it is properly an attribute of Absolute Being as such.

In the existential or moral order, there is no such thing as intrinsic evil in the sense of absolute and inescapable evil. What is called intrinsic evil in moral writings is merely that which, in the mind of the author and considering the circumstances, cannot possibly be imagined as having any good effect. Evil cannot be used as an absolute term since there is no possible human action the nature of which could be purely, intrinsically, absolutely evil. The only such act would be the destruction of absolute good, which is impossible.

Evil, then, is relative and circumstantial. Even within those limitations, there are some deeds which will always remain opposed to the dignity and destiny of man — not because they are intrinsically evil, but because they are existentially incompatible with a rational animal's proper use of life.

The notion of intrinsic evil is a false absolute, and its imprudent use may lead to erroneous conclusions and embarrassing reversals, as for instance in the case of usury.

St. Thomas Aquinas declared: "To take usury for money lent is unjust in itself, because this is to sell what does not exist." [5] Something unjust in itself is intrinsically evil. Either St. Thomas made a monumental blunder, or he was speaking relatively, in the light of his own information and of his own time, in which case he was right: in medieval days, money was not a commodity, and loans against interest were then mere

[5] *Summa Theologica,* II, p. 78, a. 1, concl.

extortion. The injustice was relative, and only those who had insisted on taking it absolutely were embarrassed when they were forced to change their views.

The same applies to the Church's insistence on the intrinsic evil of contraception. In earlier days, no good was seen to come from sexual acts from which procreation was formally and intentionally excluded. A lesser world population and a much higher rate of mortality demanded a greater effort toward fecundity. The situation now is the exact opposite, and yet the Scholastic emphasis on the procreative function of marriage is maintained by all conservative churchmen, who rely on arguments that are pessimistic, exaggerated or obsolete. Besides the fear of widespread sexual license, an existential argument, the backbone of the whole conservative theory consists in the statement that contraception is obviously opposed to the natural law. This is obvious only to those who are steeped in a static, *a priori* notion of man and woman and refuse to take into account the actual lives and sufferings of individual couples. No solution may be offered by sweeping declarations embracing every possible case and founded on the natural law, for there is here no clear and objective element of determination. Had the solution been that simple, we would never have witnessed such widespread divergences as those that now exist between wise and well-informed authors on both sides who all claim to hold the true Catholic view.

The true natural law is absolute and immutable. Every moral consequence deriving from it will enjoy the same character of absoluteness and necessity. Since every ruling on sex proposed by the traditional school is proposed in the name of the natural law, it may seem to have a claim to immutability. The next thing to do, then, is to analyze this claim by checking the validity of the principles on which it rests.

The key to the problem may be found in the position taken in regard to the procreative or non-procreative use of the semen. According to traditional teachings, any sexual act in which the semen is not given full opportunity to originate a

THE NATURAL LAW

new life is intrinsically evil because it is opposed to the natural law. No other reason than that is ever given for the immorality of contraceptives, withdrawal or pollution. Let us consider now how absolute is this natural law in the minds of those who elaborated the rules of sexual morality. The following is a text by a seventeenth-century theologian:

> Concerning touches implying a risk of pollution: The premises are, first, that voluntary pollution is always intrinsically forbidden, and that, by natural law. See for instance Thomas Sanchez, *b. 9, d. 17, num. 15,* and Lessius, *bk. 4, ch. 4; ch. 3, dub. 14 and passim,* and the chief reason usually brought forth in defense of this truth is that, if pollution were permitted, it would prevent the normal use of marriage so necessary in the world: for if men were content with this pleasure alone, they would not devote themselves to their marriage.[6]

This text leads to three important remarks:

– Pollution, or the induced loss of semen, is said to be intrinsically evil when it is sought as an end in itself and results in eliminating the procreative effect of sex. The loss of semen, then, is intrinsically evil only if procreation is intrinsically good, which is a fallacy. This means, not that masturbation is good, but that it does not belong in the category of automatic mortal sins in which traditional moralists, almost unanimously, have placed it.

– The second point is that the chief argument against masturbation would now militate in its favor. What the world needs at present is precisely the opposite of what it needed then: instead of underpopulation, we now have overpopulation.

– The third and most important point is this: in those days what was called "natural law" was not seen as an immutable principle of human nature or divine will, but merely as a matter of historical, mutable circumstances; to wit, the needs

[6] *Explicationes in Decalogum,* Thomas Tamburinus, S.J. (Lyons, 1659), vol. 2, p. 72, par. 46.

of the world at a certain moment of history. If the whole structure of norms concerning sexual morality rests upon a natural law the naturalness of which is mere expediency, there is not the slightest contradiction in changing the norms according to the demands of the time. If what theologians have meant all along by such expressions as "intrinsically evil, by natural law" amounts to nothing more than "practically evil, by historical necessity," then when the necessity changes, so must the norms — and this without impairing in the least the edifice of immutable truth.

This seems to open a door in the cage in which theologians have entrapped themselves. By giving an absolute character to the declarations on sex, they have been misinterpreting earlier teachings on the matter, adding to them a rigidity that appears entirely unjustified. Instead of a change in attitude being a reversal of the position of the Church, it will be nothing more than a return to the common sense from which some of its teachers have strayed, often out of excessive zeal and concern. It is much easier for a few theologians to admit they have been too strict than for the whole Church to confess it has been wrong.

Because of rigidity in the teachings concerned with spiritual life, there is a frequent loss of contact with nature, and hence with the neighbor, who is nature at its highest. Many a stiff condemnation will necessarily involve a loss of love; for love is the full participation in what is the gift of self, with no concern for legalism. The true spirit of love is in total contrast to negative mortifications and sacrifices carefully accounted and catalogued, which lead the soul to a desert where life is reduced to concern for one's own salvation. In this land, it is all too easy to build castles of unreality, made up of sterile thought piled upon sterile thought, and to live in them in total blindness and contentment for having refused to let in the world of pain and passion. The most vital and natural feelings of mankind are crushed by rigorists in a rage of salvation that leaves nothing but ruins. Marriage is treated with the same heavy-handed approach as other things that happen to be inaccessible to certain minds. Instead of respecting everything good in nature and man, in the natural dignity and symbolism of great religions, and in the natural dignity and religious symbolism of sexual love, rigorists brush all this away in the name of some unreal and formalistic notion of perfection, born of the bad Western habit of reducing the undefinable into mental categories within which living reality is forced to fit in Procrustean fashion — as if living reality, with its myriad leaves and flowers, could be compressed and packed into a perfect cube, and then divided into sub-cubes which are labeled A to Z! Try reading this dreadful sentence in a single breath, and you will have an idea of its author's anguish, and of the difficulty of any attempt to eradicate Gothic churches from Siam and notions of Gothic chastity from the Jansenistic mind.

A century and a half before Christ, Terence had written: "I am a man, and nothing of man is foreign to me." Those who fail to realize it come under fire from Claire Pichaud, a contemporary French poet and singer: *"Malheur à vous qui croyez être purs, et qui gardez vos corps comme on garde son champs!"* ("Woe to you who believe you are pure, and who guard your bodies as one guards his field!")

Gothic chastity is based on a series of false, misleading or approximate notions. They are that sex is dangerous, that it is an unfortunate necessity for the continuance of the human race, and that any other method of reproduction of the species would have been better, the ideal being the self-perpetuation of the male untroubled by female temptations. *Sex, then, is under* a priori *suspicion;* it cannot be permitted to yield explosive natural joys; *it must be controlled severely* and reduced to the lowest possible level and used only for its main function of reproduction. If everything sexual is somewhat tainted, *virginity is automatically holy.* Such are the premises of all classical treatises of moral theology.

An accurate expression of the natural law of marriage must get rid of all three assumptions and begin with a statement of their exact opposite: Sex is a good gift from God that greatly enriches those who use it properly in both its reproductive and personalistic functions; there is a virtue and an obligation of gratitude in taking full advantage of it; finally, as we shall see later, virginity is a superior vocation only for those who are called to it.

The moral laws of sex, inadequate as they are, cannot be brushed away: they must be developed and pruned of many obscure and pessimistic accretions. When one considers the jungle of fears and false beliefs of the average man and woman in matters of sexual right and wrong, the need for a serious cleansing becomes obvious. Non-Catholics often argue that the Church does not understand human love. They are mistaken, but even Catholics may object with good reason to the manner in which basic moral principles are sometimes expressed by old-fashioned counselors who seek to restrain vice but succeed only in creating a repulsive image of virtue.

When those officially endowed with the magisterium of the Church clearly fail in their obligation to define and promote moral truth, it becomes everyone's duty to enlighten them and bring them back to a sense of reality. The current rigoristic view of sex, entirely male, celibate, abstract, deductive and a priori, has lost contact with the dynamism of actual life. Its teaching, innocent of any reference to real married people, is a syllogistic exercise based on static definitions of man and woman. That it happens to be right on many points is a happy coincidence rather than the result of valid reasoning. Whenever it is wrong, the error is but the result of inadequate premises.

Once again, what is needed is not a mere alleviation of a few disciplinary laws, but a reversal of attitude: the elimination of scornful male spiritualism in favor of a comprehensive love for the male/female complex considered in its dynamic role in a universe advancing toward the Pleroma. The full flowering of mankind consists, not in the fabrications of uneasy minds afraid to face the reality of sex, but in the encounter with this same reality elevated to its true significance. Man and woman and their love are the signs of that love which is God, and it is through them, through respect for man as man and woman as woman, and for their true love as the highest human act, that humanity will make its symbol come true, being then living love in the closest possible union with the living God.

AN EXISTENTIAL-PROGRESSIVE VIEW

Such a conception of the true value of sexual love demands a corresponding theology and an adequate expression of the rules of morality. There is no reason to start from scratch by denying the value of the very notion of natural law: far better to accept it as the immutable foundation of true morality in a way that will differ from the conservative attitude only in the elimination of dead wood and the growth of new and more natural leaves.

A full flowering of sexuality for individual men and women implies four stages:

1) *A study of what sex is,* of its male and female aspects as originally created by God, its means, and its goal.

2) *A consideration of the positive value in oneself of the sexual tension,* seen as a powerful springboard of emotional and creative life.

3) *An acceptance of sex as an interpersonal relationship* destined to develop both partners in the conjugal union of body, heart and soul.

4) *An offering of sex as a way to God* through the flowering of the mutual gift, the perpetuation of life and relationship within the communion of saints.

These four stages are not drawn from a preconceived notion of man, but coincide with a realistic response to the challenge of individual destinies.

There is much more dignity in the rational education of freedom than in the drilled-in habit of obedience to rules that are seldom understood. The saint is not the man who obeys blindly, but the one who sees his personal road to God so vividly that he is able to follow it in the full clarity of his intelligence and with the full consent of his will.

In this light, much prejudiced rigidity disappears, much of what was seen as "unnatural" becomes relative, and over-emphasis on sexual sin is unmasked as an obsession. When the ideal consists no longer in conformation to authoritarian rules but in doing what is right for one's existential perfection, many problems become matters of fact rather than of prin-ciple. Of course, it is important to maintain the objectivity of true personal perfection: it is not a fabrication of ours, but free adherence to God's will; something perhaps not actually preplanned, but at least preordained directionally, and the direction is not for us to choose, but to follow, so that what is right for us should not be confused with what is most pleasurable.

The theology of sex must be rebuilt, beginning with the inner reality of the person of Christ. If young lovers could be made to realize that their love originated from the Father, is expressed in the likeness of the Son, and results in the fruits of love itself and in the child, as the love of Father and Son results in the Spirit; if only they could know that they were created out of love, for the sake of love, and with absolute Love as their end; if they could realize that the reality of the presence of Christ within them is more real than they are to themselves — then they would regulate their own personal rela-tionship, not as a mere means of pleasure nor as a matter of commands and prohibitions, but as a free participation in a constant ascent.

What is this fact of man in which Christ is dwelling? Man is an ever-perfectible being, a conscious continuum living in the midst of change, seeking his own development through every power that he is. There is in him no such thing as a moaning and perfect spirit held down by the fetters of the flesh, nor is there a glorious flesh tyrannized by a misunderstanding spirit. Man is flesh-and-spirit, a brother to the incarnate Christ. Because of his complexity and imperfection, he is a yearning and unsatisfied whole seeking his perfection in the fulfillment of his unity, while attempting with the help of grace to overcome the original damage done directly to the spirit and indirectly to the flesh. This human complex which must be elevated to perfection comprises different drives: upwards to the absolute, but also horizontally in time and space through every legitimate avenue opened to its spirit of unrest.

Since it is only indirectly and by accident that the body is vitiated, not everything done with the body is sinful and wrong as such, as some heretics believed, but a number of those things may fall short of order and harmony. Perfection, then, will consist not in the exaltation of the spirit at the expense of the body nor in that of the body at the expense of the spirit, but in a conscious and disciplined attempt to mend the broken order and harmony by letting each faculty and function play the part originally assigned to it. In other words, man is not made of two parts, a top and a bottom, so that it would suffice to exalt the one and ignore the other in order to attain perfect sanctity and happiness. On the contrary, man is an "informed body" or a "received soul," so that he cannot function properly without a mutually dependent body and soul, the body providing the vessel and instrument of life and the soul its motor and principle.

It is this whole complex, inhabited by Christ, which performs the act of love. Moral virtue and perfection apply to this act because it is much more than a physiological phenomenon: it is the result of a free and rational encounter of two persons united sacramentally, involving not only their bodies but also their hearts and souls, and affecting directly both family and society, of which it is the source. And so it is good by nature, by natural right, by the law of human necessity, and hence also by virtue of t' e natural law. It is good, not because the Church tolerates it as a gesture of condescension toward

human weakness: it is good in itself as a glorious expression
of human love, and the Church has nothing to concede about
it. Its goodness is not one of the treasures which the Church
may hand out by making it depend upon some ritual, nor is
it something more or less imperfect which the Church condones
through its blessing. On the contrary, it is so clearly distinct
from the power of the Church, so naturally above being con-
ferred by it, that the ministers of the sacrament of matrimony
by which the right to the act of love is granted and made holy
are not the priests of the Church but the parties themselves.
Nor has the Church the right to scorn the married state, as
it has done so often through its theologians, and even through
its saints — who were canonized for their virtues and not for
their mistakes: "The way of life is twofold, the one lower
and more common, that is the way of matrimony; the other
angelical and the highest, that is, the way of virginity." [7]

Since, however, the marital union has extensive consequences in terms of morals and salvation, the Church, although
unable to bring it into being, has an undeniable right to a
reasonable control of its conditions and use. In this sense,
and in this sense alone, the Church is the legislator in charge
of the elaboration and publication of the moral law of sex,
which it must establish on the basis of that reality which
is man.

The natural law must be expressed, not in the form of
abstractions, but as existential propositions adapted to the
here and now of every human couple, and comprising human
destiny as a whole. Individual moral good is *the dynamic
state of a rational animal seeking the Beatific Vision through
the proper use of its temporal life.*

The yardstick of all morality, and not only that of sex, must
be its relationship to the constant ascent of man toward Point
Omega — his existential end. For those who do not fully realize
that their ultimate goal is the Beatific Vision, the distant and

[7] St. Athanasius, *Epist. ad Amunem,* PG, T. 26, 1174.

absolute fulfillment may be replaced by closer objectives: human dignity, the development of human powers, the flowering of personal love, and others. But total wisdom implies awareness of these immediate objectives and also of their ultimate fulfillment in eternity.

Applying these general principles to sex, it seems that any use of it which conforms with personal love, with the development and enrichment of the partners within the context of their existential vocation is morally good. Being directed toward both procreation and mutual support, any use of sex, provided it procures close companionship, increases conjugal love and is pleasurable to both parties without impairing the general procreative end of marriage, is at the same time good and meritorious. What needs to be defined and clarified is not a series of acts, but the principles of perfection leading to man's vocational ascent.

VI

Religious Celibacy Versus Marriage

"Who would dare to judge whether they are equal or different in rank when it comes to receiving heavenly honors?" ST. AUGUSTINE

The title of the present chapter intentionally reflects one of the misconceptions most often found in manuals of moral theology: the notion that there exists some kind of formal opposition between the religious and the married states, and therefore some necessary difference between the degrees of perfection attainable. Because of the unfortunate distinction between the "state of perfection," or religious chastity and the "state of imperfection," or marriage, we are constantly being told that perfection is found in the religious state, while marriage, although admittedly good, is not the best.

It may be claimed, perhaps, that the enormous majority of celibates among canonized saints is a sufficient proof of the superiority of their state. This, however, is begging the question, for their vast number has a very simple and human explanation: with the greatest candor and consistency, ecclesiastical authorities have been honoring those of their own

70

kind, while reluctantly admitting for canonization a few married men and women — these have usually been duly cleansed by a period of widowhood.

The comments of the *Roman Martyrology* in the case of St. Rita of Cassia are characteristic of the general attitude of churchmen: "St. Rita, a widow and nun. . . . who, after being disengaged from her earthly marriage, loved only her eternal spouse Christ." [1] There is nothing wrong, of course, in loving the eternal spouse, but cannot this be done concurrently with a measure of warmth for the deceased husband? The brush-off is definitely crude. In the entire history of canonized saints in the Latin Calendar there is not a single example of recognition of wedded love since the time of Christ. Mary and Joseph are honored because of their virginity. The fact that Peter was married is carefully kept in the dark. Many martyred couples are honored — for their martyrdom. There is an exception in the Greek calendar, where the parents of St. Basil the Great and St. Gregory of Nyssa, SS. Basil and Emmelia, are remembered as a couple.

This may have been the result of a medieval conspiracy against married love fostered by the spirit of Gothic chastity whose best-known victims, Héloise and Abelard, seem to have been mercilessly and brutally hounded even after their passion had received the sacramental blessing. To find a respectful recognition of ideal marriage, we must go all the way back to Christ at Cana and to the pagan myths of Philemon and Baucis, of Hector and Andromache, Ulysses and Penelope, Orpheus and Eurydice. Why? Has there never been heroic sanctity in the married state, precisely in its perfect fulfillment?

How did sexual activity ever come to be associated with damage, loss, pollution, stain, filth, sin and so forth? Certainly in the early Church as in most pagan cultures there was no such violent prejudice: sex was taken much more simply as one of man's natural functions. The only explanation for all

[1] Westminster, Md.: Newman, 1946, p. 110.

the holy horror seems to be the proximity of the sexual organs
with the excretory, so elegantly pointed out by Augustine.[2] It
is the unfortunate privilege of Patristic Christianity to have
developed this fact into a doctrine debasing both sex and
marriage.

As for Christ, no man would ever dare to judge. But, should
the life of Christ be seen as absolute proof of the superiority of
the state of virginity? In him there were present both perfect
virginity and perfect maleness, combined in total harmony.
He lived in the midst of women and loved them perfectly. As
a man, he must have known the longing of natural desire, since
he possessed the fullness of male sexuality. But for him the
state of virginity and perfect chastity was the only one compatible with his function as the Savior of mankind. Being perfect, he could practice perfectly both spiritual and physical
continence. As the Master of Perfection and the Sun of Justice,
all he ever did was as humanly ideal as could be. This does not
mean that he was so much above the human condition that no
temptation of the flesh could have assailed him: on the contrary, he was so close to us that he experienced all of our pains
and hungers. The only difference is that he did not yield to
them, when yielding would have been sinful or imperfect. Does
this mean that the state of Christ is a condition of perfection
for every man? It would only be so if every man were the
Savior of mankind, the Son of God and the Second Person of
the Holy Trinity.

Saint Bonaventure makes an interesting distinction between
those acts of Christ that are to be imitated as being those of a
perfect man, and those that cannot because they are the acts
of God.[3] Some of the things Christ did cannot be imitated by
man because of sheer impossibility: his miracles, for instance.

[2] *"Inter faeces et urinam nascimur."*
[3] *Defense of the Mendicants* (Paterson, N.J.: St. Anthony's Guild Press,
1966).

Others must be imitated: his deeds of meekness, truth and love. In between the two there seems to be an area where the desire to imitate Christ absolutely may very well be presumptuous because it implies superhuman strength and grace. A life of total continence is one such thing. I am not saying that perfect chastity for the love of Christ is impossible: I am only suggesting that it is possible to none but those who are very specially called to it and who take full advantage of the graces that accompany their calling.

What of Luke 20:34–36? "The children of this world marry and are given in marriage. But those who shall be accounted worthy of that world and of the resurrection from the dead neither marry nor take wives. For neither shall they be able to die any more, for they are equal to the angels, and are sons of God, being sons of the resurrection." (Confraternity version.)

Does this mean that Christ proposes virginity as a condition to the fullness of the reward in the life to come? Not in the least. Christ is answering here a question by a Pharisee about the woman who had had several husbands. When she dies, of which of them shall she be the wife? He answers that married persons in the next life will no longer be tied by the legal bond, so that the fact of the woman having been married several times is irrelevant. Many arguments may be used in defense of this interpretation.

The third sentence: "For neither shall they be able to die," etc., clearly refers not to virgins but to married persons after death, since virgins have not been relieved of the liability of death: "they" shall not be able to die, not because they are virgins, but because they are already dead and now enjoy eternal life; "they" are equal to the angels, not because they are virgins, but because now they have joined the choir of spirits singing God's praise.

The French "Bible of Jerusalem" makes this interpretation very clear, for it reads: "Those who shall *have been* [qui *auront été*] accounted worthy," indicating that the judgment is already past, and that reference is made not to living virgins but to dead spouses.

The corresponding passage in Matthew 22:30, clearly says: "*At the resurrection* they will neither marry nor be given in marriage." And Mark 12:25 reads: "*When they rise* from the dead, they will neither marry nor be given in marriage."

Finally, St. Bonaventure in his *Soliloquium,* speaking of the joys of heaven, has this to say: "There we shall be like the angels of God, if not in age, at least in happiness." The reference is obviously to the three passages quoted here, and the expectation of happiness is not restricted to virgins.

And so, when Luke 20:34–36 is quoted in defense of angelism and as supporting the identification of "virgin" with "equal to the angels," as so often found in Eastern hagiography, it is a clear case of misinterpretation of the Gospel.

The use of sex, then, is a loss only to those who are called to the imitation of Christ's chastity. It entails no damage, stain or pollution whatsoever in those whose supernatural vocation is marriage—even when its use implies erotic refinements and sensual delights. On the contrary, there is here a meritorious gift, a mutual perfecting that comes about through sexual fusion.

Whence, then, the negative rantings of ascetics? Once a man has set out to prove that the one and only perfect way of life is that of total continence, it is natural for him to call this state "purity." The married state then becomes "impure." Whatever makes the difference (that is, the physical act) is called unclean. Thus, a confusion is established between the sin of uncleanness, which is sexual abuse, and the act of sex itself. The simplest way to defend ascetic practices is to attack marriage and sex. That this has been done with perseverance and ferocity may be seen in the dreadful accumulation of negative ecclesiastic writings, some samples of which have been given above.

Such aggressiveness can be understood only as a desperate

effort to overcome inner doubts. When every rational form of logic has failed to prove one's own superiority, nothing remains but authoritarian dogmatism. With the prejudice of the absolute perfection of virginity enthroned as a dogma, and in the absence of supporting evidence either human or divine, repetitive assertiveness had to be resorted to, together with thunderous condemnation of sex. And the usual manner of this condemnation consisted in heaping abuse upon woman and seeing in her the cause of pollution and perdition.

To be sure, this is no longer the view of the Church. Yet, much of what is written now by moralists is tainted with the same spirit of arrogance and intolerance. In such matters, even tolerance is unacceptable, for there is in sex and marriage nothing to be tolerated or condoned: marriage is in itself and of itself a holy state, not in spite of sex but precisely because of it, because of the glory of the sexual union of man and wife in the name of the Father and of the Son and of the Holy Spirit.

And speaking of purity, what greater purity than that arising from the cleansing fire of true and mutual love?

When we look beyond the negative interpretation of certain texts from the Gospels and Epistles and search the fountains of doctrine, it becomes clear that the Church in its wisdom forbids only this: to hold that the state of religious celibacy is *not* the highest. It is certainly possible, then, to hold that the state of religious celibacy is indeed the highest, but only in the abstract, and that in the concrete the highest form of life for any man is that to which he is called. This is not contradicting the declaration of the Council of Trent, but drawing from the distinction between the abstract and the concrete a natural consequence which has been pointed out by others before.

If a vocation is a call from God — and marriage surely is a vocation — then it is inconceivable that God would have called the majority of men to a state which is inferior by necessity, thus by an act of his will depriving them of any chance of obtaining the higher rewards. God is certainly free to favor certain souls, but how could he will to prevent the largest part of humanity from attaining the level of perfection, and reserve this level for a minority?

This matter has been clarified once and for all in a letter addressed by Pope Pius XII to Bishop Charue of Namur, Belgium, on July 13, 1952. Bishop Charue had consulted the Pope on the question of whether the life of the regular priest was more perfect and generous than that of the secular. The Pope answers that, in fact, it is not even more perfect than that of the layman.

Speaking of the state of perfection the Pope writes:

> Thus it is not the personal perfection of the individual which is under consideration. This is measured by the degree of love, of "theological charity" which has been reached in him. The criterion of the intensity and purity of love, according to the Master's words, consists in the fulfillment of God's will. Hence the individual is personally all the more perfect before God as he accomplishes more perfectly the divine intention. In this matter, the state in which he lives is of little importance, be it lay or ecclesiastical, and, for the priest, be it secular or regular.

In perfect accord with this teaching, Father Henry V. Sattler writes:

"Once the individual has finally chosen (a state of life), that state is the way to heaven for him. All discussion concerning the relative value of the different states in life ceases when that decision is made, for in the concrete, the best vocation for each person is the one to which he is called." [4]

The same notion is developed once more in the Constitution *De Ecclesia:*

"All the faithful of Christ of whatever rank and status, are

[4] *Parents, Children and the Facts of Life* (Paterson, N.J.: St. Anthony's Guild Press, 1952), p. 64.

called to the fullness of the Christian life and to the perfection of charity." [5]

This precisely proves my point, that there is no *a priori* concrete superiority or prerogative belonging to anyone in any state. Providence expects of each man an individual and unique contribution to the kingdom of God. Each man, then, will attain his own individual perfection within the framework of his unique calling.

For a man strongly called to the married life, the religious state could not possibly be the highest: he would live in it in a mood of dissatisfaction and frustration, not, as so often assumed, because perfect chastity is too lofty or too demanding for him, but because he has been called to something else which, in his particular case, may be even more lofty and demanding.

To put it in simple words, many an excellent and successful family man would have made a very poor priest, and many an excellent and holy priest would have been intolerable as a family man. To every concrete, real, actual human being, the way of perfection is his concrete, real, actual state of life. For the religious, it is the state of religion; for the married, it is marriage. The highest mansions of heaven are open to every human being, for there is no bar to them besides sin, and no condition besides love.

It follows that marriage, considered as a true Christian vocation, implies no diminishing of religious ideal, no renouncing of any higher reward, no loss of any prerogative or special rank in heaven. It is not the religious as such who will enjoy the highest place, but the saint — and every man is called to sanctity. And perfect marriage, with its countless labors and heartbreaks, its constant demand for total sacrifice, its daily practice of poverty, chastity and obedience, is a better way to perfection than many a moralist ever suspected.

What indeed is religious poverty — as currently practiced in

[5] Par. 40.

an institution where all the necessities of life are amply and assuredly provided — compared with the poverty of a family man who is never sure of meeting next month's food or fuel or housing bill? Religious chastity is undoubtedly a great virtue, but what of the sacrifices demanded of man and wife who must live in the closest intimacy and yet so often abstain from the full expression of their sacramental love? And has there ever been a religious superior so uncompromising, so demanding, and expecting such absolute, constant and tyrannical obedience as any baby?

The constant emphasis in religious writings on the physical fact of virginity and the lyrical exaltation of it are more than mere exaggeration: they are signs of a serious misunderstanding of virtue. Virginity as such is merely a negative state that may be developed into a virtue. The conditions are that it be entered upon for the sake of greater love, and that it produce fruits of greater love. For virginity to be virtuous, it is not enough that it be entered upon for the sake of avoiding the dangers of sex. Obviously also virginity is far from virtuous when it results in nervous tension, psychological storms, bitterness and obsessions — or even in the smug belief that the physical fact alone entitles the virgin to a position of privilege and honor in this world and in the next. In all such cases, far from being a virtue, virginity is a detestable habit, both unnatural and damaging. It is unnatural, for when nature is neither satisfied nor elevated to supernatural love, it turns into the subhuman; and it is damaging, for it hurts both the subject in which it produces unrest and the neighbor who suffers from that unrest.

There is a great difference between disparaging the sacrifice of the true virgins and establishing the claims of virginity in proper perspective. Many holy men and women, in the full knowledge of what they are doing, renounce forever the joys and consolations of sexual partnership in an act of splendid dedication to God. They are fully deserving of our esteem and respect, and they should not be offended in the least by what is written here. There are many mansions in heaven, and theirs will be of unspeakable splendor. Others, however, consider sex as a catastrophe to be avoided at all cost. They may be in perfect good faith, supported as they are by an all-too-abundant array of ecclesiastic writings. It is their thesis — not their persons — that this work is opposing.

The position taken here cannot be considered anticlerical in the sense of being offensive to the clergy, but only in the sense that it tends to counteract a certain usurpation of power and competence by the clergy. The clericalism it opposes is that condemned at one of the sessions of Vatican II by Bishop De Smedt of Bruges, Belgium, in his now-famous trilogy of the Church's ills: "Triumphalism, legalism and clericalism." As a South American bishop pointed out in another session of the Council, "There would be no anticlericalism if there had been no clericalism."

A clear instance of the uneasiness of religious writers before the problems of sex is their general consternation when faced with the fact of the holy married priests of the Eastern Rite. It seems to some Latins that the whole universe of Western spirituality is crumbling, when in fact nothing is destroyed but a prejudice. There is a great difference between a respectable tradition and a tenacious error. Truth is based, not on antiquity, extension, or frequency of repetition, but on objective conformity with fact. A notion is true, not because many have endorsed it for many years, but because it happens to conform with reality. Remember Galileo!

The major mistake, the historical blunder under which we are still suffering, is the inference that perfection, identified with virginity, is irretrievably destroyed by the sexual act. When sexual consummation is seen as nothing but a pollution of the body and a loss of virginity, the whole picture of wedded life becomes clouded. Such a notion is so persistent that it still crops up in the works of contemporary writers. For instance, after quoting the most devastatingly negative and obsolete opinions, Father Joseph E. Kerns, S.J., summarizes their teaching by saying: "Abstinence from sexual intercourse is associated with nearness to God." [6]

Why is it so hard for these good men to realize that sex is part of human nature and that it is in no way an obstacle to union with God, except in its distortions? And distortion consists not only in the excessive pursuit of sexual pleasure, but also in an unbalanced appraisal of its function. There are sex deviates who distort the act. There are many, too, who distort the notion by either exalting or debasing it irrationally. They then go out as preachers of laxity or preachers of rigidity and spread their personal brand of folly with all the zeal of false evangelism. There are probably more Comstocks than Casanovas — and it is questionable which one of the two groups has done the greater damage.

Abuse of the act of sex is generally a sin of weakness; abuse of its notion is always a sin of pride, and is much the greater sin. Excessive exaltation makes of Eros a god; excessive debasement makes of him a beast, leaving the virginal onlooker to believe himself a god, or at least an angel — and this on the strength of judgments that are necessarily secondhand and of principles that are often completely wrong.

There is yet another disturbing aspect to the question of virginity. Its contradictory definitions provide an unedifying example of theological vacillation:

> Virginity is irreparably lost by sexual pleasure, voluntarily and completely experienced. . . . This perfect integrity of body, enhanced by a purpose of perpetual chastity, produces a special likeness to Christ, and creates a title to one of the three "Aureolae" which theologians mention.[7]

[6] *The Theology of Marriage* (New York: Sheed & Ward, 1964), p. 122. The tone of the whole work is disturbingly negative. "However great his good will, however high his ideals, he [the married man] is starting down a road which will keep confronting him with what might be called 'urgent trivialities,'" one of which, undoubtedly, is giving birth to more joyful theologians!

[7] "Virginity," Vermeersch, *Catholic Encyclopedia* (New York, 1913).

The special virtue we are here considering involves a physical integrity. Yet, while the Church demands this integrity in those who would wear the veil of consecrated virgins, it is but an accidental quality and may be lost without detriment to that higher spiritual integrity in which formally the virtue of virginity resides. The latter integrity is necessary, and is alone sufficient to win the aureole said to await virgins as a special heavenly reward.[8]

These two incompatible definitions are found in the same work. Both, however, are impossible to reconcile with a view expressed more recently by Bishop Fulton J. Sheen:

With Christianity, virginity ceased to mean physical intactness, but unity. It meant not separation but relationship, not with the will of another person alone, but also with the will of God.[9]

All Christians — and not the religious alone — live, if they choose to, as an image of the Word, in the name of the Word, and with the Word as their final goal. But they also live in close relationship with every expression of the Word available and accessible in daily life. They live, if they choose to, in a state of awareness of the metaphysical splendor of all existing things; they know that to exist is to be loved, and to be loved is to be in the likeness of God. They know that they themselves are one of the highest forms of this likeness, that they are loved not only as beings but also as persons, and that this personal love is the supreme goal and completion of their life. They know that this their love will be achieved through the perfect fulfillment of their personal calling, be it lay or religious. And they know, finally, that, in whatever state they are called to live, they may see and enjoy the splendors of God's creation: in the religious life, the beauties of nature, art, intelligence and human friendship; in the married life, these same marvels with the specific supplement of participating in God's creative power not only in the spirit but in the flesh.

[8] "Chastity," John W. Melody, ibid.
[9] *Three To Get Married* (New York: Dell, 1961), p. 129.

There is, then, no real difference or opposition between the two ideals, religious life and marriage, since perfect religious life leads to the deepening of the whole man or woman, while perfect marriage leads to spiritual love.[10] There is no contradiction that would put them in opposition to each other, since the religious life may be adorned with natural graces, while the married life may be steeped in a living sense of God, and both the religious and the married are in need of human contacts and affective development.

In the married state, this takes the form of mutual support of husband and wife and of perpetuation of the human race, both functions being performed through the same vital expression of love. Since the essence of the married state consists precisely in the right to the full union of the sexes, it is plain nonsense to teach that such union should be "spiritualized" by eliminating all passion, or that there is no virtue in full and uninhibited liveliness of sexual relations. Yet, such is often proposed by authors of pious works who are afraid of the explosive glory of physical life; timid souls who, having denied it to themselves and having no faith in it, would also deny it to everyone else.

In the religious life, sexual emotions and desires — which cannot be eliminated by any effort or any form of penance for the simple reason that they are part of human nature — may be humbly acknowledged and directed by sublimation to the proper end of this state. A man or woman utterly and absolutely deprived of any means of affective expression or any source of affective enrichment by complete severance from their sexual complement will live in a condition that is both unnatural and harmful. For there is in both man and woman a vital need for some kind of recognition and tenderness on the part of the opposite sex. The very sacrifice implied by perfect chastity

[10] Constitution *De Ecclesia*, Par. 32: "The distinction which the Lord made between sacred ministers and the rest of the People of God bears within it a certain union, since pastors and the other faithful are bound to each other by a mutual need."

makes no sense, as we have seen, if it consists merely in rejecting the "evil of sex." In order to be meritorious, it must consist in the fully conscious surrender of some good.

Even in the state of perfect chastity, there remains the need for some kind of mutual assistance which makes the difference between bitter, frustrated isolationism and the harmony of a complete human being. The sexual need is always present. Repress it, dam it up, and like a mighty river it will rise, break the dam and go on a rampage, brushing away conventions and decency. At the very least, it will change life into a maze of obsessions, scruples and self-torture whose external effects will add a drop of vinegar to the most virtuous work. On the contrary, be aware of it, see it as a constituent element of human nature, feed it gently with tenderness and respect, and it will flow peacefully between its banks enriching every passing hour.

Sublimation differs from repression in that, instead of brushing off the problem, it faces it squarely. Sex, then, is seen as a good worthy of sacrifice. In true sublimation, the goods of husbandhood and wifehood, as also those of fatherhood and motherhood, are recognized as highly valuable in their natural form, but replaced by methods of expression of a different order. They are universalized and spiritualized, extending beyond the confines of a single family so that they may reach out to the whole Mystical Body of Christ. They apply not only to those related by the ties of blood, but to all those who come with their various needs and beg for assistance and love within the framework of the particular assignment of a priest or religious. The same sublimation applies in a sense to the married, for their love should transcend by far the family circle and enclose all of mankind in its care and concern.

The final word, as always, belongs to Christ:

"At that time the disciples came to Jesus, saying, 'Who is the greatest in the kingdom of heaven?' And calling to him a child, he put him in the midst of them, and said, 'Truly, I say to you, unless you turn and become like children, you will never enter the kingdom of heaven. Whoever humbles himself like this child, he is the greatest in the kingdom of heaven'" (Mt. 18: 1-4).

"'. . . whoever .wishes to be first among you shall be your servant; and whoever wishes to be first among you shall be the slave of all'" (Mk. 10:44).

"'For everyone who exalts himself shall be humbled, and he who humbles himself shall be exalted'" (Lk. 14:11).

 **VII**

Angelism and Anti-Feminism

"Qui veut faire l'ange fait la bête." BLAISE PASCAL

Angelism, as we recall, is a form of exaggerated spirituality that places all the blame for sin and imperfection on the body. It is a natural consequence of Manichean and Platonic dualism and of the overemphasis on virginity; it is a denial of the fundamental unity of the human complex.

In attempting to destroy the worlds of nature and natural happiness under the pretext that they may lead to sin, there is no great achievement of virtue, but only a sign of weakness. There may be greater danger in the pride of angelism than in the abuse of natural functions — in spite of a widespread belief to the contrary. Pride is the major sin against charity and the deepest opposition to love of God and neighbor, while sexual sins, adultery excepted, are seldom more than defects in fortitude and self-control. Scorn for what is good on earth will never lead to the possession of what is good in heaven. There is need for conversion in the natural order, for the proper placing of natural goods, before any progress is possible in the order of the spirit. It is the whole man, body and soul, that must rise progressively through a properly balanced recognition of all human values.

The course that steers away from all pleasure is no more

secure than any other. On the contrary, it may lead to the presumptuous notion that natural consolations are superfluous,
and end up in lands of winter harshness, of inflexible rigidity
toward self and neighbor — and to a way of life that is more a
living death than the loving ascension it was meant to be.

Blaise Pascal had angelism in mind when he wrote, "*Qui
veut faire l'ange fait la bête.*" His saying may be understood
in two different senses, both of which are illuminating. It
means first that a man who tries to be an angel — who attempts
to live above the human condition in a state of scornful isolationism which he believes to be the summit of spiritual virtue —
is prone to fall, through pride and the effects of inhibition, to
the lowest level of the subhuman. But it also means, in a more
human and humorous sense, that a man who tries to play the
part of an angel succeeds only in making a fool of himself.

In spite of being so clearly erroneous, angelism seems to
have had a number of followers who completely misunderstood
the true nature of perfection. Instead of accepting their humanity with its sexual characteristics as a fact, good or evil
according to the use they made of it, several overly conservative religious groups labor under the delusion that sexual attraction and fulfillment are a tragedy, and that the only proper
thing to do is to build up a wall of defense. They consider sex
God's greatest blunder!

Until quite recently, in a certain North American seminary,
theological instruction on the sixth and ninth commandments
had to be reserved for the last year of study, *after* ordination.
Not a word had been breathed about this dangerous subject,
except in the form of vague and horrified condemnations of the
flesh and of the sins of lust. When the fateful day of initiation
finally came, the young priests solemnly filed into the class-
room, wearing cassock and stole. After a sprinkling of holy
water, they were armed to meet the devil in person. Duly
exorcised, they sat in dead silence and befitting awe before the

professorial desk on which two tapers had been lighted. The master in person, usually a monk of advanced age, then rushed through the reading of the official commentaries, hemming and hawing at every embarrassing word. And that was that. The young priests were now fully prepared to go out into the world, hear confessions, and give authoritative advice to married people on the most intimate details of their life.

This indicates a complete lack of simplicity, an obsessive fear, an unhealthy repression, when all that was needed was a measure of common sense: the teaching of sexual matters whenever the occasion arose, instead of reserving them until the very end as the final and supreme abomination.

This same spirit leads to ludicrous extremes. Fear of sex and of the sense of touch is sometimes so great that, for example, in another seminary students were actually forced to use wooden paddles to stuff their shirts into their pants! Such insanity is now rare, but the instruction of many religious in matters of sex is still definitely obsolete. There is need of a tempest of fresh wind to cleanse the official teaching.

The frightfully strict recommendations so often addressed to novices would make sense only in cases of sexual obsession. The point is, however, that such obsession may very well be originated and developed by a secretive and horrified approach. Those with a true vocation to religious chastity have no need for rigoristic warnings: they abstain, for natural or supernatural reasons, from anything improper without having to be thundered at. Those who do need severe warnings either do not have the vocation to chastity, or have been infected with unhealthy curiosity precisely because of unhealthy methods of teaching.

It is high time that those in charge of schools and seminaries prepare in their students a proper ground for the flowering of virtue instead of encouraging the growth of such a jungle of inhibitions and guilt complexes that it takes not only ordinary grace but a near-miracle for the young religious to preserve his natural balance. This may not be true of all seminaries, yet the fact remains that such was the doctrine received and accepted by many a priest now in a position of authority.

As a corollary to angelism, there is anti-feminism, which assumes many forms. The reader of theology manuals may become so immune to the official leaning that he no longer notices the constant emphasis on the masculine and a corresponding lack of consideration for woman. This is the consequence of a long and sad tradition which began with antiquity and was accepted in part even by St. Paul.

In the first chapter of *The Triple Way*, a mystical treatise, St. Bonaventure lists among the bodily favors perfecting nature "integrity of limbs, a healthy constitution, and the dignity of sex." This seems fine. What a good thing to find the notion of dignity associated with sex in a medieval work! Alas, it is not so: the context clearly indicates that what the good saint means by "the dignity of sex" is the favor of being masculine, of not having had to suffer the indignity of being a woman!

The great Bossuet, in his *Elévations sur les mystères*, writes complacently: "She [woman] was, in the order of the body, but a portion of Adam, a reduced model so to speak."

In the Old Testament, there is even an indication of the comparative monetary value of man and woman: " '. . . When a man makes a special vow of persons to the Lord according to your valuation, then your valuation of a male . . . shall be fifty shekels . . . If the person is a female, your valuation shall be thirty shekels' " (Lev. 27:2-4). This is obviously not of divine origin, but part of the human and social element of the Bible.

There are countless other examples in literature. As recently as in the 1963 session of the Council, a female newspaper reporter was refused communion in St. Peter's, apparently for no other reason than that she was a woman.[1] Perhaps the official

---

[1] *America*, Nov. 16, 1963.

in charge had in mind the question seriously debated by medieval theologians, "whether or not woman has a soul" — and did not feel quite safe about the answer!

With very little concern for the state in which woman had been placed by the pride of man, early theologians had seen her, not as the victim of male lust and arrogance, but as the temptress whose charms were used by the devil to make man lose his superior perfection. Nowhere in medieval writings does man seem to be scorned for being the seducer of woman: with touching constancy the guilt is placed on the other sex. For woman, the loss of virginity is an unfortunate accident; for man, an intellectual and moral catastrophe. This is in complete contrast with later attitudes, for instance the nineteenth-century "double standard," illegitimate affairs being condoned in the case of men but severely condemned in that of women. In neither system does the woman win: in the medieval view she is accused of being an instrument of the devil; in later times, she bears the moral and physical burden resulting from male incontinence.

No wonder intelligent women feel frustrated and even insulted. Although much of what is written of man in theological works applies to bisexual mankind, there is often such a strong masculine bent as to be definitely embarrassing. When, to the natural superiority complex of the male, there is added that nagging anxiety which women inspire in rigidly ascetical minds, the result may be most discouraging to the feminine reader.

Nor is there much comfort for women in the lyrical praise addressed to the Mother of God, for most of it, at least in the Western and Latin literature, is offered not to the mother but to the virgin. Christian mothers, then, are made to feel that they possess neither the dignity of the male nor the privilege of the virgin. The flowers they receive from clerical authors are seldom better than consolation prizes, slightly wilted leftovers for those who did not quite make the grade.

More consideration must be given to the positive value of

woman, to the full glory of her specific perfection as a lover and mother. For woman is not the passive instrument of procreation planned by the Scholastics, nor is she a toy for the pleasure of man: she is a full and equal partner in life and love — worthy of greater honor for bearing in her flesh all of the consequent pain.

Anti-feminism, like angelism, is still rampant in some religious institutions. In the Near East, for instance, the novices of a religious order of men are forbidden to see or talk to a woman, even their own mothers, for fear of contamination by the dreadful temptation of sex. These young men are not destined for a cloistered life: they are to go out in the world after their years of formation — or deformation — in the seminary. They are to be let loose, in fact, in a world in which half the people they will face will be women.

An extreme form of anti-feminism is practiced by the monks of the Eastern Rite in the Orthodox monasteries of Mount Athos, where everything feminine or even female is so strictly forbidden that no ewes or hens, no female cattle or fowl of any kind are permitted to cross the boundary wall. Here is the very limit of unreality, the logical outcome of such an outrageous misunderstanding of sex that it is made to appear as the supreme occasion of sin. Here also is an application of the childish principle that anything unpleasant can be eliminated simply by ignoring it — as if a fundamental human instinct could be totally repressed without danger.

The extent of the phobia appears nowhere more clearly than in the text of the official imprecations hurled at any member of the "satanical sex" who would have the misfortune of setting foot on the Holy Mountain: she would instantly be "separated from Father, Son, and Holy Spirit, the consubstantial and life-giving Trinity, struck with the curse of the holy fathers, and punished with the anathema fulminated by the assembly of the just."[2]

[2] Cf. "Mille ans de vie monastique," J. Decarreaux in *Etudes* (July-August, 1963), p. 120.

One wonders what Father, Son and Holy Spirit think of this treatment of their beloved daughters, and how all this can be reconciled with the lavish cult of the Mother of God.

But this is not all: in terms of misogynic insanity, it is the Coptic monks who take the cake. Some of them live in monasteries on the small islands of Quebran and Dag-Stephanos on Lake Tana, at the head of the Blue Nile. It has been told that during a recent storm a boat loaded with men and women capsized close to the island shore. The monks waded in and helped the men to land — but the members of the dangerous sex were piously left to drown. And they did.[3]

Traces of sex phobia may also be found in pietistic literature. Such false ideas as the linking of sanctity with flight from anything feminine — or, in the case of women, from anything masculine — are so prevalent even in our days that this grave distortion of common sense and reality is praised by the hagiographer as a jewel in a saint's crown of glory. It has been written with great seriousness — and read with proportionate edification — that St. John Berchmans, a Flemish Jesuit canonized after an early death, never looked his mother in the eye, and that while being suckled he never set hand on his mother's breast, a gesture considered highly unbecoming for a future saint, and even somewhat obscene.

This is the same spirit that caused the solemn and ridiculous terror of certain Anchorites who derived a quixotic pride from victory over temptations their own distorted imagination had inflamed: they blamed the devil for their own psychoses. Such men who seem to have devoted more time to self-torture than to the love of God are manifestations, not of the spirit of the Beatitudes, but of the exhibitionism of the Fakir.

True asceticism is all well and good as a positive virtue. It consists, not in panicky flight from anything sexual, but in the well-ordered capacity to give up the good for the better

[3] Cf. "Le Christ aux sources du Nil," Louise Weiss, in *Plaisir de France* (Christmas, 1963), p. 11.

in the line of one's personal vocation. It implies a, true and delicate sense of values, attained through education and personal culture: through the comparative study of all manner of goods, including those of the earth, and through a process of perfection of all that is worthy of man, including the gift of sex.

To be sure, religious asceticism and virginity are of great value when used in their proper context; there is no doubt that nature is very much in need of control and of the assistance of grace, and that the religious ordination and vows convey sufficient and even superabundant grace for the preservation of physical, emotional and spiritual integrity. But it is also true that grace should find a response in a properly prepared nature — and that much of what has been described in the preceding pages leads to the exact opposite. Crippling views such as these must be eliminated, not only because they are erroneous, but most of all because they offer a repulsive image of religion. Whatever makes Holy Mother Church ugly and unattractive is undoubtedly evil and therefore foreign to her — for the true Bride of Christ is all-pure. Some of the errors concerning sex were seen to be affecting fallen-away branches of the Church. Many, however, are still hurting her very children.

In the Gospels, there is not a trace of anti-feminism. On the contrary, Christ Himself during his public life was constantly surrounded with women who served him and loved him, and whom he loved and helped in the most perfect way. His attitudes toward them — toward his Mother, toward Martha and Mary, even toward Mary Magdalen and the woman taken in adultery — was one of kindly interest and concern, the re-action of a man in his maleness to a woman in her femininity. He showed loving courtesy when he bowed to his mother's wish at Cana, charitable reproach for Martha's lack of judg-ment, all-embracing compassion and pardon for the repentant sinners. How, then, could scorn for women be taken as a sign of perfection?

ᨌ VIII

The Sins of Sex

"A physical act of love which does not begin in
the soul is a living lie."   CARDINAL SUENENS

As we look around us, the impact of original sin on our daily
lives is readily apparent. What is this sin, so mysteriously
symbolized by the eating of a single fruit, which instantly
destroyed innocence and order and established instead the
reign of sorrow, shame and death? The mind reels in horror
at the thought of what it must have been: a cataclysm sur-
passing every concept of fallen man. The main reason why we
are unable to comprehend its gravity is that we cannot visualize
the elevation and splendor of the state of innocence which we
know by revelation to have existed at first. As with the fall of
Lucifer, the fall of man was so great because he tumbled from
such a lofty height.

But what, precisely, was the nature of this action? Was it
motivated by a desire of the flesh or of the spirit? The Scriptures
point clearly to an act of pride and disobedience which had to
do with a breach of man's obligation toward God, and not with
the abuse of any physical power. The material punishment for
a sin must not be confused with the sin itself: If Adam and
Eve were ashamed and covered up their nakedness, we should
not jump to the conclusion that they were covering up the

organs of their sin — a deduction made by several medieval theologians and some contemporary moralists.

Because of the fall, the mind became prone to accept compromise, the will to seek imperfect good, the senses to bypass the control of reason. Inordinate desires were born — the craving for illegitimate pleasures of every kind, both of the spirit and of the flesh. But since of all the cravings of man those of sex are perhaps the loudest and most universal, and their abuse the most frequent, concupiscence — a general term expressing the disordered state of the will in relation to satisfactions of any kind — came to be associated almost exclusively with sex. So much so that some theologians did indeed propose the theory that original sin consisted in the fact that Adam and Eve had made use of their sexual powers before the time appointed by God, thus vitiating forever the source of life and of the deepest physical pleasure.

Once the seeds of misunderstanding had been sown, they took strong root. With this prejudice in mind, some moralists, observing the almost universal sinfulness of the use of sex in their days, became convinced that the act was evil, and came out with preposterous statements such as those quoted in the chapter on Negative Sources. Their mistake consists in having built up a partial truth to the stature of a dogma — an instance of the sophism marked by passing from the relative to the absolute. Their error may be seen easily when the reasoning is expressed in the form of a syllogism:

An act that necessarily implies shame and guilt is evil.

Sexual intercourse, as far as we know, seems always to imply shame and guilt.

Therefore, sexual intercourse is evil.

The conclusion is an absolute statement which obviously exceeds the content of the minor: no absolute conclusion may be drawn from a relative truth based on the examination of a limited number of apparent facts.

Even if in all the cases observed there had been doubtless shame and guilt, no absolute conclusion could be drawn, but only this: that there was evil in those cases that were actually observed. This leaves the door open for intercourse without shame or guilt.

What is rightly condemned in the Scriptures is not the act as such, but depraved nature in its propensity toward disorderly pleasure. What was corrupted by the fall was not sex, but the disposition of the will toward it. The flaw is not in the act of love, but in the intention of seeking pleasure through it without regard for the moral law.

A sexual sin consists in a rebellion, not of the flesh against the spirit, but of the whole man against the purpose of his God-given power. Through sexual sin, man becomes more and more inclined to destroy himself and to compromise his eternal beatitude for the sake of some passing and incomplete delight.

Every sin is a cleaving to what is not good enough. The sinner is maimed to a greater or lesser degree, the greatest harm being done by Luciferian pride, through which the creature prefers itself to God. A sin, although always formally present in the will, may be of the mind, of the heart or of the flesh. If the mind goes astray, there may be absolute refusal to accept the light of truth, and this leads to the sin against the Holy Spirit and to the darkness of despair. There may also be a refusal to accept one particular aspect of truth, and this leads to the dusk of compromise. On the level of the heart, there may be either aloofness, leading to the unreality of a closed and frozen universe; or a scattering of affection right and left, leading to vanity and exhaustion. On the level of the flesh, there are possible abuses in the choice of partners and in the aberrations of the act itself. Since man meets woman on all three levels of will, mind and heart, it is on all three levels that he must attain order and preserve integrity before reaching any degree of perfection in his union with her.

There is in our time a twofold phenomenon: while in too many minds sin is automatically associated with sex, yet the frequency of sexual sin is so great as to eliminate almost entirely the notion of guilt. The supremely illogical reasoning seems to be: if sin is found in sex alone, and there is no real guilt in sex, sin is a mere fiction and there is no reason for restraint. The consequences of such reasoning are everywhere present.

A clear case of identification of sin with sex may be found in the expression: "He lives in sin." This does not mean that the man is a monster of pride or a murderer, that he exploits widow and orphan and all who work for him, that he spreads heresy among the gullible and corruption among the innocent, that he is scornful, uncharitable or brutally egotistic: it means merely that the poor fellow goes to bed with a woman who is not his wife!

Why should a sin of weakness, a personal and private sin the judgment of which certainly does not belong to the neighbor, be so often treated as the supreme crime? Perhaps it is made to be so by hidden envy on the part of the gossiper, or by easy self-inflation over the neighbor's fall. Perhaps, also, the sensitivities of many are so blunted as to allow them to become immune to crimes too great for them to comprehend — such as colossal pride, genocide, or social injustice, disguised under the false labels of glory, power, or nationalism. More probably, there is here a remnant of the theologians' ancient terror that sexual union may be the lowest act of man and its abuse the most degrading evil. On this point, alas, the modern gossiper would have the support of Thomas Aquinas, and, in terms of the number of those in hell, that of Alphonsus Liguori and several others.[1]

We should take our sinning a little more seriously. Except in cases of adultery or monstrous abuse, the sin of sex is often a mere lack of fortitude. This does not mean it is not grievous: on the contrary, since it is ordained toward an end "that is bigger than both of us," and touches upon so deep and funda-

---

[1] *Theologia Moralis*, n. 413; quoted by Aertnys-Damen, *Theologia Moralis* (1919), vol. 1, p. 251. Also Toletus, *In Summa*, 1, 5, cap. 13; Isidore of Seville, and many others.

mental an aspect of the human person, its guilt is proportionately severe. And yet it has many degrees, ranging from the slight imperfection of some passing voluptuous thought to devouring possession by the demon of lust.

There are two possible excesses in matters of conscience: coarseness and hypersensitivity. The habit of seeing mortal sin everywhere is an effect of such hypersensitivity, which may turn into crippling scrupulosity. The overstressing of mortal sin may also lead to the weakening of the notion of sin itself, furthering the natural tendency that we have already observed. If a man feels that a mortal sin awaits him at every step, he will become discouraged and be tempted to give up the fight entirely.

In the sexual relationship, there are some few single acts that are directly and absolutely fatal to the soul; there are others that induce a state of progressive death, in the sense that a soul that sinks repeatedly into the same bad habit ends up by turning itself away entirely from God's will. The grave matter in this case is not the act itself, but the deadly disposition of the will. The death of the soul, then, and its liability to eternal punishment depend either on a single act of such gravity as to make a man or woman forfeit their every chance of enjoying the Beatific Vision, or on a succession of acts resulting in a vicious habit by which the will, in the full light of the intelligence, seeks time and again its own pleasure in direct defiance of God's law. No one damns himself without knowing it and willing it, but he can do it either piecemeal or at a single blow.

The confessor's problem is not easy. In the impersonal encounter of the confessional, the penitent is generally unable to give a sufficiently clear and objective picture of his action to serve as the basis of an accurate judgment. In many cases, the penitent is quite unable to analyze his own motives. Even if he can, he may have great difficulty in expressing them. In fact, then — and this is not a disparagement of the sacrament of penance, but merely a factual observation — many sinful acts are estimated by the confessor, not on their real motivation, but on their face value alone, and the counsels addressed to the penitent have the same inadequate foundation.[2]

As a consequence, because of the gravity of sexual sin, and in the absence of any clearly expressed extenuating circumstance — and perhaps also because of the confessor's justified anguish before the flood of sexual abuse — many penitents acquire a distorted belief that every stepping out of line in matters of sex is automatically a mortal sin. Even a thought, a passing glance at some desirable object, the sudden emotion before human beauty, the hunger for close physical companionship may throw them into a state of terror as if this were enough for their soul to be condemned to eternal death. Not that any confessor would tell them so, but the general severity of ecclesiastic condemnations would induce them to believe it.

And so, while it is a fact that the sins of sex often lead to very serious guilt, it is also true that obsession with this guilt leads to an overextension of the notion of mortal sin — which in turn deprives many souls of contact with the Church and with those very sacraments through which they could have obtained their healing.

Like any other sin, sexual sin consists in a failure of love — more precisely, in desiring or performing the act of love in the wrong circumstances of partner, place, time or manner; in the disordered choice of taking for absolute what is but relative pleasure; in the search for one's own gratification as an end

---

[2] "In sexual matters it is altogether impracticable, if not actually impossible, for confessors to try to draw the line between inordinate instinctual desires and truly human needs." "Marriage Questions," *Contemporary Moral Theology,* John C. Ford, S.J., and Gerald Kelly, S.J. (Westminster, Md.: Newman, 1963), vol. II, p. 231.

All such matters are left to the individual conscience properly enlightened, and to God's mercy, that is, as Bonaventure expresses it, "to the One to whom it pertains to attend to questions of weight, number and measure in matters of guilt, pain and intercession." *Breviloquium,* VII: in fine (Paterson, N.J.: St. Anthony's Guild Press, 1963), p. 288.

taking precedence over the dictates of natural law. It is the violation of a function so sacred that any trespassing is almost sacrilegious, for it damages the wholeness or holiness of life and accomplishes the negative miracle of turning into obscenity and filth one of God's glorious gifts.

Extreme misunderstanding of this gift leads to the notion that sex comes, not from God, but from the devil — a notion so persistent in art, in literature, and even, as we shall see, in advertising copy, that nothing short of a searing bath in the fire of truth could eradicate it from the depths of prejudiced minds.

Although the satanic origin of sex has no foundation in reality, examples of such a belief abound. Early paintings and engravings in the style of Breughel the Elder and Hieronymus Bosch represent the gates of hell as a distorted and gaping vulva, and many a similar reference could be quoted from medieval folklore. There is much worse: satanism and sex have combined in abominable rites that are still being performed. Knowing the Father of Lies for what he is, there is no wonder that he has taken advantage of one of man's most dynamic instincts and turned it into a means of sacrilege.

The effects of satanism on man's appreciation of sex are certainly deep and enduring. They may even lead to complete revulsion for the sexual relationship. They also explain in part the negative attitude of religious writers. The question, however, is not whether sex may be used for the perpetration of crimes, but whether sex properly perfected may lead to the acquiring of merit. To take everything sexual as a suggestion from the devil is to play into his hands and to insult God who created the man-woman complex for the delight of his children and the propagation of the human race — and thus as an instrument of his eternal glory.

The spiritual remedies against the sins of sex are actual grace, prayer, and the frequent reception of the sacraments. The practical remedies are the proper understanding of love and the regular practice of self-control. Self-control needs to be built up progressively in every domain of human pleasure, for the unbridled pursuit of even the mildest satisfaction will necessarily turn into excesses in the greater. And love must be properly learned and practiced, since it is the essential constituent of human nature, metaphysically and emotionally speaking. Were it not for God's love, we would not even exist; and were it not for some form of affection, we would die of emotional starvation.

Because love is so much part of man, the deepest and most vital expression of it has an explosive power which may be channelled for better or for worse according to the measure of discipline of the lovers. Too many give up before even trying. Overwhelmed from the start by a powerful instinct, encouraged by a society lacking in sexual understanding and restraint, too many surrender their will in the first encounter and fall prey to temptations as fast as they come. They bow to the defeatist principle that "It can't be done," that chastity cannot be preserved and that control is beyond the power of human nature. In this they are partly right: full control of sex is in fact beyond the control of nature *left to itself*. But to give up in advance is a grievous form of despair. God's help is always available and effective.

It is possible to kill the conscience; it is impossible to fool it. A dead conscience reduces a man to the state of spiritual death, a state to which he condemns himself and in which he will remain forever unless he frees himself through repentance and atonement. Any pleasure sought and obtained in such a state is the pleasure, not of a beast (for a beast cannot sin), but of a rational being driven by an evil spirit, which is much worse than had it been that of a beast. It is not only subhuman but in a sense truly satanic: for no living action is possible without a moving spirit, and, when the spirit of love is dead, the door is left open to the spirit of hatred. Pleasure is then ever-fruitless, ever-deceiving. It may often result in suicidal despair, as statistics show in Sweden, the land of free love. When all the powers of man are directed to what is below him, to what is not, to a nonexistent absolute, the contrast between the allness of the spurned God and the nothingness of the chosen object results in mental, moral and physical torture.

As long as the conscience is not dead, it remains sufficiently vocal to spoil the fun of any guilty sex play. For it remains as a nagging voice, perhaps not during the fleeting moments of ecstasy, but certainly forever after, building up complexes of anxiety that are the very antithesis of satisfaction.

The sin of sex often bears its own punishment in this world. It is the waste of something that could have been so much better, the spoilage of a fruit before maturity, the scattering of a power whose fulfillment is found but in a single holy union. As every sin of sex spoils the mental and affective attitude of illegitimate lovers or of those married lovers who abuse their right, so every act of rational discipline and restraint opens vistas of delight upon a love that is still to come. In this, as in all things, virtue and happiness coincide, provided virtue be understood in the open light of true sexual freedom; and such coincidence occurs, not only in the heavenly Jerusalem, but often and quite surprisingly right here and now.

Sinner and saint alike seek but one thing: happiness. The sinner, by flouting the laws of God and expecting freedom from them; the saint, by obeying the laws of God and finding freedom in them. And even in terms of downright lively, enchanting, erotic delight, it is the saint who wins.

IX

Birth Control—Observations

> "If ecclesiastics would not command us to believe
> as oracles of the third heaven the imaginings of
> Scholastic theology, the sects would then return
> to peace."   WITZEL

It is strange that to so many minds the problems of sex and
marriage have been reduced to that of birth control, as if it
were all important, and as if its practical solution could resolve
every other difficulty. This is putting the cart before the horse,
for the question of birth control can be solved only after a true
and complete doctrine of sex and marriage has been clearly
developed and existentially accepted.

The proper attitude toward the rules of the Church in matters of moral law is one of respect and obedience. This does not
exclude the right to personal thought, nor the fear that all at
present is not as well as it should be. The days of blind confidence in everything and anything published in the name of
the Church are definitely over: we may now ask pertinent
questions and expect rational answers.

The conservative position of the Church as regards positive
contraception has been explained in countless books and pamphlets. It is under serious fire from several quarters. As presently formulated, the Church's position is based on rules of
sexual morality that would apply with great logic and accuracy

to couples of low vitality, culture and imagination, having no children or too few, living in an underpopulated area, and willing to choose between almost complete continence (the very negation of their state) or a system of charted and artificially timed intercourse which is both ineffective as a means of control and destructive to married harmony. To put it simply and straightforwardly, the conservative system is completely theoretical and unreal.

How can the consciences of spiritual guides remain unmoved before the increasing flow of sincere and anguished testimony, before the spectacle of the hundreds of thousands, perhaps even the millions, of marriages being led to slow decay by obedient compliance with artificial rules? Sociologists of the future will marvel at the docility with which Christian couples let themselves be pushed around by masters of immense good faith and proportionate incompetence whose anti-sexual bent has tended to deprive the spouses of their sacred and God-given intimacy.

The complete unnaturalness of the conservative view appears clearly when we consider the results of perfect compliance with its dictates. After a long period of frustration and sexual starvation, which is most painful but has value in terms of both merit and discipline, a young man finds himself a wife. Long before husband and wife have attained any measure of sexual harmony, the first child is born. Then comes a period of sacrifice, tiredness, common effort and adaptation without any sexual compensation. Many weeks after delivery, they are supposed to be free to resume their intimate relationship. But are they? If they do, children follow, year after year, exhausting both mother and father and posing a possible threat to the children already born. So they are told to practice rhythm. This leads nine times out of ten to chaos in their emotional lives, not to mention unexpected babies, the natural result of the chances involved in the practice of "Vatican Roulette." The wife labors for years in order to bear children and bring them up. As long as pregnancies are desired, she may have some measure of sexual satisfaction, but she is probably too tired to make the most of it. As soon as her maternal duty is fulfilled and pregnancies become potentially catastrophic, fear robs her of all freedom in her sexual life. Instead of being rewarded for her generosity by an increased enjoyment of sex, she becomes so nervous and frigid as to be almost totally deprived of it — and this by complying with authoritarian decrees supposedly based on nature!

After years of confusion and dissatisfaction, both partners are so thoroughly fed up with their calculated and artificial relationship that they lose all interest in the ecclesiastic version of the love game. They drift apart and may be strongly tempted to seek compensations elsewhere. And so, perfect obedience to the conservative laws of sex results in the very opposite of natural harmony and moral virtue.

One of the consequences of virtuous living is the warm and comforting glow of a good conscience, that peace of mind which is the equivalent of a moral pat on the back and remains as an encouragement not to stray from the right path. This peaceful glow is totally absent in those who fully obey the present laws of marriage and use no other limiting method than rhythm. If they are not purely passive, if they are endowed with any amount of rational sense, they perceive doubt and unrest, they are pursued by the nagging thought that, after all, their hardships and sacrifices might not have been necessary — or that many of them could have been foregone without impairment of their virtue and with a considerable increase in their happiness. The penitential and redemptive value of past sacrifice is not in question: any act of obedience, based in good faith upon a command of the Church, retains its quality of merit. But once a command is seen to lack any rational foundation, and obedience leads not to peace but destructive unrest, what reason is there for further compliance? Even St. Ignatius of Loyola's celebrated formula of obedience, *perinde ac cadaver* ("as passively as a corpse"), excluded any violation of conscience. When a law is clearly seen to be wrong and its error is confirmed by the practical damage entailed by its application to real life, there may seem to be greater immorality in obeying it than in disregarding it.

Pope Paul VI, however, has requested all Catholics to obey the traditional rules as long as they have not been officially revised. Yet it is perfectly legitimate to study the question very closely and to suggest the elements of a necessary reform. This may take the form of pertinent questions.

Why, for instance, should it be necessary that lovemaking always maintain the possibility of procreation even when a new birth is unreasonable, undesired, and even a potential evil? The purpose of any organ is subject to the needs of the whole body. After the duty of fecundity has been fully satisfied, or when there are grave reasons not to increase the population of a given area, the maintenance of fertility in sexual relations is definitely harmful to the persons involved or to society.

Some good souls may be shocked by the notion that there is at times a *duty* of avoiding pregnancy. They would argue that such would amount to reducing the number of the elect. This is not the point at all. By limiting the number of births, we are not preventing anyone from reaching heaven – as if there were billions of unborn souls in some outer-space cage waiting for us to liberate them, and who would be thwarted by our lack of generosity. This is nonsense. No harm can be done to a nonexistent being – although it is all too easy to sin against the fruit of love. Once a child, even an unwanted child, has been conceived, it is a good of immense value, fully endowed with the right to live. But if, in order to maintain the level of world population, to safeguard the health and sanity of overburdened parents or provide a minimum of food and education for their children, further pregnancies must be avoided, this should be done legitimately through *rational* means.

The present system results in a tremendous increase in the size of families in destitute areas and underprivileged nations. Obviously the blame cannot be placed on the Church alone: a large share of responsibility rests with society, national and international, which is answerable for flagrant inequalities in the distribution of food, wealth and opportunities. Little of the blame can be placed on the underprivileged themselves. It is easy to accuse them of excessive sensuality and lack of control. The reasons why they have so many children are of an entirely different order. First, they cannot afford the contraceptive tricks of the rich. Often they have never even heard of them. Also, it almost seems that undernourishment leads to an increase in fertility — as if nature compensated for the loss of life due to hunger by increasing the number of those born. Finally, the natural joys of sex are the only consolations left to the poor. In the act of love alone, they regain for awhile their lost human dignity.

The point is very well made by Archbishop Roberts: "A typical case: an Indian lives in a mud-hut with his wife and several children, too poor to be able to afford any light and forced to be with his wife every night for twelve hours in the dark and having nothing else at all but love."[1] The Archbishop then goes on to cast serious doubt on the validity of the official position condemning all methods of positive control.

What many couples of good faith are concerned about is not the search for gratuitous sexual pleasure. They are perfectly willing to have children, sometimes even lots of them. They refuse with perfect human right to bear a twofold burden: the care of children *and* sexual starvation. They object most logically to being forced by rules — much more artificial than contraceptives — to abstain from the expression of their love in most of the few instances left to them. After carrying the weight of life, of married life with its crushing responsibilities and obligations, made heavier by the acceptance of their fecundity, these couples have only too little strength and too few opportunities left for love.

Human nature being what it is and the sexual urge being so

[1] *Search* (London: Michael de la Bedoyere, April, 1964), p. 445. Cf. also Bishop Roberts' Introduction to *Contraception and Holiness* (New York: Herder & Herder, 1964), p. 19, in fine.

strong, there will necessarily be within marriage a great number of acts having every possible reason not to result in pregnancy.

Let us now examine in detail the different methods by which the limitation of births may be obtained.

Intercourse in which mechanical devices (including diaphragms, condoms, suppositories, jellies, foams, etc.) are used cannot be considered ideal because of their frequent lack of esthetic or psychological acceptability. The least objectionable of these, however, should be considered in the light of the principle of double effect, *and not rejected as intrinsically evil.*

As for "the pill," there is a twofold problem, one of fact and the other of principle. Has it been sufficiently tested to be proved safe? If safe, can it be used morally, and when?

Doctor John Rock's endorsement of the pill is easy to understand: he is dedicated to the problem of relieving human suffering. Having contributed to the development of the pill, he is also convinced of its effectiveness and harmlessness. But is it possible at the present point to share his optimism?

I fail to see how any considerate husband, after reading the medical literature on oral contraceptives in their present state of development, can still expect his wife to use them. It seems that few doctors recommend them to their own wives, except under their careful and constant supervision. The dangers may certainly not be exaggerated, since the medical reports are published by the manufacturers whose main interest is to sell their products.

Now, what do these reports say? Oral contraceptives are contraindicated for patients with heart or kidney diseases, breast or genital cancer or hypertension. They are not recommended before a thorough test of endocrine functions; caution is recommended in cases of patients with metabolic disorder (including diabetes), migraine, epilepsy and asthma. Thromboembolism with some fatalities has been noted; mention has been made of additional growth of the mother's body hair, showing a modification in secondary sexual characteristics; and there have also been cases of inversion effects on the sexual characteristics of the female embryo. To this list must be added the findings of independent physicians who noted the following aftereffects: mental depression, nasal irritation, shrinking of the uterus, skin diseases, and possible brain damage. Recent reports infer the danger of induced blindness and other possible damage.

As of now, there is no certainty that every woman using the pill will not have to suffer in her flesh, or that her offspring will not suffer, because of imprudent tampering with the natural equilibrium of fundamental physiological processes.

All this is definitely frightening. One advertisement frankly states: "The use of X for more than three years must await the result of continuing studies," a clear confession that the long-range side effects of oral contraceptives are not yet fully known. It will take a close study of the lives of thousands of women and of their offspring to determine with any degree of accuracy how safe the new drugs actually are.

Some major questions remain unanswered: Can ovulation be prevented again and again with total impunity? Can the delicate female glandular system be upset time after time without producing some dangerous disturbance in the long run? There has already been some indication that menopause is retarded in women who use the pill regularly.

There is a vivid contrast between these potentially serious threats and the reckless manner in which millions of women swallow tens of millions of pills like so many aspirins.

Answering the first question, then, we may say that as the matter now stands no complete, sound and final moral judgment is possible on the pill because of lack of factual information. Some moralists who have permitted its use for the sake of regulating menstruation do not seem to have sufficiently considered its potential dangers.

Supposing, now, that the medical and physiological properties of oral contraceptives were proved to be entirely satisfactory, or at least not excessively dangerous, since nothing in this world is perfect, could they be recommended for general use? In view of the urgent need for some dignified and rational means of birth control, it seems that they would be acceptable for use in all cases of legitimate sexual union in which there is no good reason to favor procreation. They could not be resorted to as a method for the procuring of unlimited and irresponsible satisfaction of the sexual instinct, in extramarital affairs, or even in marriage, for moderation and restraint will always remain necessary — and even some periods of total abstention, as recommended by St. Paul for the sake of prayer. A medically safe pill would be acceptable only when intention and circumstances were right.

As for the rhythm method, it is insufficiently reliable, more perhaps because of the possibility of miscalculations than because of any fault in the system itself. In addition, it generally imposes an excessive burden of pain upon married couples. In spite of the fact that rhythm is better than total continence (for the simple reason that any small measure of satisfaction is better than none at all), it seldom offers more than a limited and disappointing means of sexual expression, and this for several reasons.

First of all, since the "safe" days coincide by physiological necessity with the wife's greatest nervousness and irritability, which immediately precede the menstrual flow, there is in the whole cycle no time when circumstances are less conducive to a happy and relaxed encounter. Most husbands know only too well of premenstrual listlessness, backaches and general allergy to any kind of exercise!

Again, because so many women have irregular periods, the actual safe zone is often narrowed down to so few days that the chances for a successful meeting within such tight margins are very slim. Since the time is known in advance to be too short, the result may be damaging anxiety, or the cramming of too much lovemaking within too few days. This not only fails to correspond with the natural frequency of desire: it also damages the quality of the encounters themselves, which suffer the consequences of fatigue and repetition. On the other hand, were the natural spacing of desire to be observed, making of each experience the joyful celebration it should be, no more than two or three encounters would be possible each month — obviously a starvation diet for lovers with any ardor in their blood.

Finally, the rhythm system implies calculations and preparations which totally eliminate spontaneity. Looking forward with great expectation to a given date may even result in complete failure, for any compulsion destroys the magic of love.

All these inconveniences combined lead to a completely unsatisfactory relationship between husband and wife who then carry over disappointment and frustration from month to month with ever-increasing anguish and sorrow. How seldom, indeed, do the actual circumstances of life produce in both partners together, precisely at the time when intimacies are possible, that surge of emotional and physical love which tends to sexual fulfillment! How often, on the contrary, do husband and wife face each other with a full-blooded and holy desire, only to be completely frustrated because the time is not right! They are then challenged, not by a wicked temptation, but by that very good which they have promised each other, and which they are now forced to forsake in themselves and deny to the other. By their sacramental union, they are two in one flesh, bound by the memories of past adventures together, naked before each other in the conjugal bed: and yet, because of an ecclesiastic law, they must abstain from the vital expression of their oneness.

There is no good whatsoever in the advice to dress in pajamas and Mother Hubbards, to spend the night apart, to use twin beds or even separate rooms, for besides the damage done by breaking up the couple, the imagination is ten times more active than are the senses. While there is some measure of consolation in the many possible expressions of physical love short of actual intercourse, living apart only amounts to adding fuel to the fire.

The trouble comes from the very quality of the sexual act. There is something immensely valuable and uplifting in the splendor of the feminine body transfigured at the summit of physical exaltation, such breathtaking vitality that any man who has ever been the cause of such ecstasy will necessarily long for more. The legitimate and virtuous partner of this experience is present with her full capacity for love, closer than any other, more willing than any other to serve and to please, to be the object and subject of what she and her lover most strongly desire. The banquet is set, the guest of honor has come in her most glorious robe, the wine is flowing, the music of emotions has reached its highest pitch . . . but no: lover and beloved must be left panting and weeping in the sorrow of paradise lost!

Woman, made to be the companion of man and the reward of his labors, becomes time after time the forbidden fruit and the source of devastating anguish. Such is the problem which is not solved.

There is then an urgent need for the study and approval of better means of control so that all married couples may use their free will in the choice between two different acts: those exceptional unions in which there is a hope of procreation, and the many others procuring natural joys unhampered by the terror of unwanted pregnancy. The encounter between husband and wife could then be the happy, relaxed and restoring adventure it was meant to be; and procreation – no longer the haphazard consequence of just any sexual urge – would be the formally willed effect of especially generous acts of love.

In the absence of acceptable methods of control, what will happen, and what is already happening? Except in cases of relative frigidity or heroic sanctity in both partners, there is damaging artificiality in the timing of the few permissible acts, a spoiling of the acts themselves because of the ever-present fear of impregnation, and a corresponding deterioration in the pattern of conjugal love. Instead of being a relationship enriched with the afterglow of physical and emotional satisfaction, marriage too often is a tense and frustrated union. Rhythm may at times change the best of wives into an anxious and irritable menstruation-watcher, totally unfit for the game of love. Its effects are harmful both to the parents and to the children, who suffer from parental disharmony. All this seems much more directly opposed to the natural law than would be a method by which sexual relationships could be rendered sterile in a manner consonant with human dignity whenever pregnancy is undesirable. In fact, however, there is at present no Church-approved means by which an ardent and fertile couple can obtain sexual satisfaction in any way proportionate to their natural inclination.

If obedience to Church laws entails suffering it does not of itself prove the laws to be wrong, but too little attention seems to be given to the torturing effects of a genuine attempt to obey them in full. Imposing continence upon married couples for extended periods of time amounts to demanding heroism from many whose natural weakness makes them unfit for such a lofty goal. The fact that Pius XII expected such heroism of all Christians in no way weakens the contention that the problem is not solved. There is no true solution when the religious counselor, after recommending continence in the name of higher spiritual values, assumes that sufficient solace is procured by prayer, devotion, and imitation of the Blessed Virgin Mary. This is a pietistic and sanctimonious approach that fails to meet the difficulty. Such cut-and-dried solutions entirely miss the point. It is not sufficient to say that a simple choice must be made between paternity and continence, for this amounts to advising the married to destroy their marriage. What if one of the partners will not agree? What of the vital and psychological needs of the couple? Not a thought is given by such counselors to the fact that, for young married people with a reasonable number of children, this would mean almost total cessation of intercourse. Who could reasonably demand of every Joe Doe, Tommy Atkins, Pierre Dupont or Ivan Ivanovich superhuman detachment from the very essence of marriage? Such harshness is totally uncharitable and unrealistic.

Few things are more dangerous to lawfulness than a precept so formulated that it cannot be observed by more than the one man in a thousand who is able to practice heroic virtue. The 999 others will have the choice between cruel suffering or total disregard for the whole system — and there is little doubt as to the choice of the majority. That is why there is such irrational cruelty in statements such as the following: "If husband and wife make use with temperance of their marital rights and live as they should, there is no fear, except in rare instances, that more than five or six children would be conceived, this being the opinion of physicians."[2]

No serious medical authority would ever endorse such a thesis.[3] The plain truth is that many a husband and wife of average fertility making temperate use of their marital rights and living as they should would end up with many more children than they could raise properly.

[2] *Moral and Pastoral Theology*, Henry Davis, S.J. (London: Sheed & Ward, 1935), vol. IV, p. 251.

[3] Cf. *An A B Z of Love*, Inge and Sten Hegeler (New York: Medical Press, 1963), p. 51:

"The chances of pregnancy resulting from sexual intercourse without the use of any form of contraceptive has been calculated as being 1 in 35."

Supposing a woman has 20 childbearing years of 52 weeks each, or 1040 weeks: if she has intercourse only once a week and pregnancy results in one case out of 35, we may calculate statistically that a child will be born on the average after 35 weeks of intercourse, to which must be added 36 weeks of pregnancy, for a total of 71 weeks. Dividing 1040 by 71, we find that she will have, not the five or six children Father Davis supposes, but OVER FOURTEEN, and this with a frequency of intercourse well below the average needed to maintain a satisfying sexual relationship.

Both the Hegelers are medical doctors, and their data, which seems to be quite recent, would prove that Father Davis' reasoning is fallacious.

The theologians' claim is a fallacy based on the misinterpretation of statistics. A medical study in support of the theory is said to have established that it took an average of three hundred acts of intercourse to bring about a single pregnancy. At first sight, the figure seems fantastically high — so high, in fact, that one wonders whether it does not include many an intercourse with contraceptives. Even supposing it to be accurate, it still provides no sufficient support for the thesis, for these three hundred intercourses represent an average, including a great number of cases in which pregnancy was physically impossible: the acts of relatively and totally infertile couples, either defective or beyond the age of fertility — many of which, having no reason to curtail their relations, probably enjoy them frequently.

Since few couples actually know their degree of fertility before it is too late to take advantage of this knowledge, all presumably fertile couples must live by the norms applying to the most fertile, and hence bear the heaviest burden of continence.

The deep wisdom and compassion of the Popes is in sharp contrast with such blind optimism. In his address to the Italian gynecologists, Pius XII showed genuine concern for this particular problem, and urged them to continue their research on the period of fertility of the ovum. There are here two major departures from earlier and stricter disciplines: the psychological and vital value of the sexual union is not only recognized but approved; and its use and pursuit are permitted even with the direct intent of avoiding conception.

X

Birth Control —Propositions

"Let there be space in your togetherness."
KAHLIL GIBRAN

Since we are faced with an unsolved problem, what can be done about it? Let us consider in turn the scientist, the moralist, and the married partners themselves.

THE SCIENTIST

The scientist's most fruitful field of investigation seems to be the natural cycle of fertility. Many studies are now being conducted in this area. As there is a duty to alleviate suffering, there is also a duty to improve and develop the knowledge of the act of love. Far from being unchristian in the sense that it would take the sacrifice out of the sexual relationship, further biological research is highly Christian in that it would relieve much pain and raise the sacrifices of Christian couples to the level of a free and willful offering, of far greater spiritual value than the present grumbling compliance with authoritarian statutes or physical necessity.

Much progress is possible, but there are also many difficulties. To mention but one, even if the time of ovulation could be accurately predicted and pinpointed in the normal cycle, there is the further point that premature ovulation may be brought about by some physical or emotional disturbance. The study, then, must bear also on the maturation of the ovule in order to determine clearly the span of its potential activity. The problem would be solved only if a test could be found to determine the exact time in which a fertilizable ovule is present – and a corresponding test to determine the exact duration of potential activity of the spermatozoa.

There seems to be no possible moral objection to medical research tending to:

– bring about mature ovulation at a given time
– prevent mature ovulation until a given time
– stabilize the interval between menstruations
– determine and analyze the circumstances leading to the production of a premature but potentially active ovule.

As a general rule, it seems that if the period of total continence could be reduced to no more than about a week, this would not exceed the capacity of spouses who both value their intimacy and are aware of the necessity of sacrifice. Such, of course, is a matter of personal vitality and ardor, greater intervals being readily acceptable to some couples, while to others even such a relatively short fast may be painful. As of today, by applying what is known of the rhythm method, some happy few may be called upon to sacrifice no more than what is reasonable and possible for them. Many others, on the contrary, are reduced to such constant hunger and frustration that their burden is almost intolerable. It is this great number which is in need of help from the scientist.

THE MORALIST AND COUNSELOR

The moralist and counselor, in turn, would do well to consider the depth of pain induced by sexual privation, particularly in couples very much alive and of great goodwill. They should try to understand the vital impact of sexual hunger on those whose sacramental state implies its satisfaction. They should be constantly aware that the present system imposes an almost impossible burden upon the married. The emphasis of their teaching should be, not on the enforcement of negative rules, but on a gentle explanation of the foundation and purpose of moral law. The stress should be placed on the necessity of defending marriage against the danger of materialistic hedonism, and on the redemptive and atoning value of willfully accepted sacrifice. Moralist and counselor should prudently and carefully repair the damage done by rigidly conservative teachings.

The conservative approach seems to be based on two principles: the sacrosanct nature of the seminal fluid, and the essential ordination of sex to procreation. So long as the sperm is free to go all the way and nothing is done to hamper impregnation, all is said to be well – in spite of the anguish and pain of those who do their best to conform with rules they obey in their will but cannot accept in their heart. What could be more obviously opposed to the natural law, to the destiny of man on earth, to his personal happiness and to the welfare of his family, to social order, common sense, logic, freedom and dignity than a system that destroys love between spouses, makes of their union a nightmare, transforms a beloved wife into an object of suffering and temptation, reduces to almost nothing the natural means of affective expression, and results in drunkenness, frigidity, severe temptations of infidelity and staggering losses to the Church? Those lost are not the lustful, but the lively; and their goodwill is often immense. At the present rate of attrition, the Church may find itself reduced to a minority group of semi-sterile Pharisees!

To consider any loss of seminal fluid as a moral catastrophe is merely a remnant of medieval superstition which saw in the spermatic flow the presence of "homunculi," miniaturized human beings implanted in the womb, where all they had to do was to grow. Since the equal importance of the female ovule was unknown, the male principle alone was granted complete reality, so that any wasting of seed amounted in a sense to murder.

There is nothing personalized or humanly living in the

seminal fluid. Furthermore, only an infinitesimal fraction of its potentialities is ever used in a lifetime. It must be treated with care and respect as the means of production of desired new life, but as soon as it has fully accomplished its function, it loses all moral importance and is nothing more than a biological surplus. It may still have some hormonal value when absorbed by the female system and may contribute to the union of two-in-one-flesh, but it has no further procreative importance whatsoever.[1]

When theologians insist on the importance of not opposing the life-producing effect of intercourse, this is all well and good in a general sense, and whenever such effect is desirable. But once this effect has been brought about sufficiently, or superabundantly, what further reason could there possibly be to maintain a power whose effects are no longer good? The only remaining purpose of sex is then the fostering of mutual love.

Have theologians considered sufficiently whether procreation is a good when the quality of intercourse is inadequate? They seem to be teaching that procreative potency must be maintained even in the most casual and imperfect matings where there is no spiritual or emotional harmony, no desire of perpetuation of life, nothing but the satisfaction of raw sensual need in its most irrational form. In such cases, is this not imposing the sin of the parents upon the child? Are not all children to be born of love? Who knows what early psychological harm may be inflicted in the first months of life (or even on a child in the womb), when a mother has conceived her offspring by accident, borne it with resentment, and then gives it birth out of sheer physical necessity and makes it pay for being unwelcome? Why should inadequate sexual acts

---

[1] "If the principle of responsible parenthood is accepted, if this principle is valid and if the couple has made its judgment in full sincerity, the biological fact of the loss of seed cannot be considered a direct sin against the primary end of marriage." Bernard Häring, *Homiletic and Pastoral Review* (July, 1964).

have to result in the much greater evil of bringing forth children emotionally and morally handicapped? Imperfect intercourse is bad enough: why must the damage be compounded? Is there not an enormous injustice in forcing irrational and subhuman relations to result necessarily in procreation? The victim, then, is the child, the unloved and unwanted child who in turn inflicts his own lesions on his descendants. This leads to a frightening chain of disorder transmitted and increased from generation to generation. So extensive is the disorder that Sigmund Freud, taking the particular for the universal, considered normal what is but the pathological effect of the sins of the parents. The Freudian monsters and complexes are neither natural nor inevitable: they are merely the consequences of Victorian prudery, wrong notions of sex, and the lack of closeness and communication between parents and offspring. They are never found in the children of true love.

Since excessive insistence on the procreative function of every act of intercourse works against order, and not in its favor, procreation should be considered, not as a universal duty nor as a natural and necessary physiological consequence of copulation, but much more rationally as the *privilege* of those who have reached the maturity required for the proper raising and education of children.

All absolutes should be removed from the notion that procreation is the essential end of marriage; otherwise there is no remedy for the problem of overpopulation. The will of God, the basis of human nature and therefore of the natural law, cannot be to make of man and woman mere baby-producing machines; nor again can it be to forbid sexual pleasure outside of the duty of procreation – since the pleasure is not limited to procreative acts alone, nor is it diminished in the least after the birth of a reasonable number of children. God's will, and therefore the natural law, tends to the fulfillment of man, woman and child – of society and humanity as a whole.

Since no amount of Church legislation will prevent people from marrying and making love, constant emphasis on the duty of fecundity will amount to worsening a difficult situation both within the family circle and in the world in general. This duty must be carefully qualified. It must be fulfilled by those capable of raising a family, and not by all. The number of children of each couple must be left to the individual conscience and determined in the light of personal, social and national circumstances.

In some instances, then, there exists a real duty of non-fecundity, which must be combined and made compatible with the universal human need of sexual expression and satisfaction. Both common sense and the natural law of human dignity seem to suggest the following principles:

– It is sinful to enjoy the pleasures of sex, even in marriage, while systematically blocking its biological outcome – but only in those cases in which the birth of a child is possible and desirable, depending on personal, social and national conditions.

– Physically, mentally or morally defective couples should not be encouraged to procreate. They may not be deprived of their sexuality nor of their power of transmitting life. But what possible objection can there be to a natural eugenics which would result from their being advised to limit their procreative effort? If ungenerous or inadequate couples wish to have no children, why not let them get away with it? Are they not dis-qualified as parents by the very fact that they reject parent-hood?

– But those couples who feel that they are able to procreate children for the glory of God and have the courage and the means to raise a large family should be encouraged to do so. Many a saint, artist and genius was the sixth, eighth or even twelfth child of a vital family.

A general solution to the question of birth control will de-pend on the application to it of the true notion of natural law; that is, it must be considered in the light of man's general destiny as a rational animal seeking the Beatific Vision through the proper use of his temporal life. Careful consideration should be given to what pertains essentially to this destiny, and is therefore unchangeable, and to possible adjustments to those rules that are merely a matter of discipline and depend upon historical and factual circumstances.

A careful study — not so much of literature as of consciences — will reveal that even at the height of conservative rigorism many good men knew in their hearts that something was awry.

The need for dynamic progress in the theology of sex is clearly shown by Father Adrian van Kamm:

> Only the leading thinkers of a religion or culture are capable of going back to the source from which their religion or culture sprang. This return to the source enables them to distinguish between what is fundamental and what is incidental in their sexual safeguards. We may call this procedure "re-sourcing." When the psycho-therapist puts up the danger sign, it may be time for a religion or culture not to deny its heritage but to return to its sources.[2]

The same need for some kind of change is expressed by a layman of great goodwill who is both a scientist and a Catholic, Doctor John Rock.

> With increasing frequency I was disturbed by the realization that the voice of my conscience was not always telling me what the priests of my Church kept saying were its dictates regarding human reproductive functioning — what was right and what was wrong in how a person willed, or permitted, or prevented expression of his God-given sexuality.[3]

To conclude: no amount of subtle distinction between interfering or not interfering with nature has any importance here, since the "nature" in question is not the immutable essence of man but the mutable actuality of the physical com-

[2] Associate Professor of Psychology, Duquesne University. "Sex and Existence," in *Insight* (St. Louis, Mo., Winter 1964), p. 8.
[3] *The Time Has Come* (New York: Avon, 1963), p. X.

plex over which man as a whole is made to reign. What counts, then, is the intention of the will. If in many instances intercourse with the formal intent of excluding procreation is perfectly legitimate and even virtuous — a principle accepted as soon as rhythm is endorsed — then the manner of this exclusion is merely of material import. Theologians are right in forbidding contraceptives, but they are often right for the wrong reasons: the present methods are inadequate, not because they prevent conception, which may be a good, but because they do so in a manner that is dangerous to the wife or may be incompatible with the dignity of the mutual gift.

It has often been said and written that any relaxation of the present laws against birth control would result in a tremendous increase of sexual abuse. Within marriage, the exact opposite seems to be the truth. Abuse is generally the cumulative effect of dissatisfaction and frustration. When the strongest natural instinct fails time after time to be fulfilled, there ensues a constant buildup of tension and a corresponding decrease in moral resistance to temptation. In other words, the sexual offender is the sexually hungry. Permission to use an effective and reasonable method of control will considerably lower the tension and urgency, thus decreasing the major incentives to abuse.

The argument that the relaxation of laws would also greatly multiply the incidence of fornication and adultery has nothing to do with its *use* in marriage. The gravity of both fornication and adultery must continue to be stressed, but the principles and methods of contraception should not be forbidden *a priori* to the married under the pretext that they may be abused by fornicators and adulterers. These methods exist and are known to all. The question is one of practical choice. It is a very serious choice, but depending much more on facts than principles. That is precisely where the traditional position needs to be reversed. "My mind is made up," says the traditionalist. "Don't confuse me with facts!"

If a perfectly good end may be achieved in marriage by reasonable recourse to methods of control, such recourse is positively virtuous, notwithstanding any vicious use it may possibly have. Every invention of the mind is potentially a criminal weapon. To forbid absolutely the use of any invention under the pretext of its potential evil is to treat every man as a would-be criminal. Such a negative and discouraged attitude cannot lead to any progress, either material or moral. A suspect already bears the stigma of crime: he has much less to lose than a man above suspicion, since his reputation is already compromised. A pessimistic view of married couples will only encourage them to commit that very thing of which they are suspected. Human frailty must be seen with realism, and yet goodwill deserves a great measure of confidence. A mentally disturbed patient, treated as if he had already achieved a certain goal, has a better chance of reaching it. If he is given up for lost, he is lost. Is it too much to assume that most married couples would use effective means of birth control, not as incentives to sexual abuse, but as means of personal development and greater sanctity?

It is hard to see how the use of a *harmless* device resulting in the possibility of the mutual gift of erotic release, in the deepening of mutual tenderness and in the strengthening of the physical bond between the couple, can fall under a thunderous anathema, while an *unnatural* and *artificial* method of calculation, leading to the exact opposite, is exalted to the high heavens. This is a direct insult to the most elementary common sense. Once again, this is an example of the classical blunder of preferring abstract principles to facts when the order of existential logic demands the exact reverse. A principle that contradicts a fact is a false principle, or, at least, a principle improperly formulated.

There is a great danger awaiting those who are called upon to reformulate the norms of sexual morality. It is due to human respect, the fear of loss of face. Now that for years so many imprudent and vociferous pronouncements have been made against mechanical contraceptives, supposedly in the name of the Church, it would take superhuman humility on the part of the rulers of consciences to admit that they had been wrong. Since some acceptable method of birth limitation has to be endorsed — otherwise an ever-increasing number of good people will abandon the sacraments and eventually the Church — there is a real threat that the anovulant pill will be approved. It is recent enough not to have been the object of so many formal vetos. Its approval, then, would appear as less of a reversal of traditional doctrines, although it is by far the most dangerous method.

THE PARTNERS IN MARRIAGE

As for the married partners themselves, they must become more deeply aware of the working of grace and of its power. Although God always provides sufficient support, it is a fact in accord with our freedom that we must ask for it and accept it; and a fact in accord with our frailty that we often fail to do so and fall instead into different imperfections — out of hunger or impatience, or out of the desire to manifest our love in that one particular way when it would have been wiser to abstain.

Inevitably, many cruel sacrifices will be demanded of those who seek to live as wisdom suggests. Besides sex, equally painful privations will be expected in such things as comfort, freedom and time. Such restrictions are accepted as a matter of necessity: why then should there not be a corresponding acceptance at least of some sacrifice of sexual pleasure? A well-balanced life is one in which pain is objectively considered as unavoidable, while pleasure is accepted with the full and grateful freedom of the children of God on those rare occasions when all is well, "when the tongues of flame are infolded within the crowned knot of fire, and the fire and the rose are one." [4]

What of pleasure and what of pain? There is a simple rule

[4] T. S. Eliot, "Choruses from 'The Rock'," *The Complete Poems and Plays, 1909-1950* (New York: Harcourt Brace, 1958), p. 96.

for combining pleasure with spiritual freedom: never to accept anything that exerts upon us such attraction that if we continued to indulge in it we would become enslaved. In other words, the legitimation of an imperfect pleasure depends upon our ability to give it up in favor of a higher good. In terms of sex, this does not mean that we should be able to stop delight at any point in the act of love, but that full enjoyment of it is permissible only when we have proved that we are its master.

There is no legitimate pleasure without some form of restraint – not because pleasure as such is wicked and needs to be held back, but simply because the economy of salvation consists in the personal obligation of every man and woman to carry his or her share of the burden of redemption. Pain and suffering are not a natural consequence of sex nor a punishment for its pleasure: they result from the general state of man after the fall. If the sacrifices demanded in a virtuous sex life are particularly hard to bear, it is because the sexual drive is so deeply and vitally embedded in human nature. The richer and more lively the desire, the greater the sacrifice will be.

The virtue of sex demands a corresponding appreciation of the virtue of continence. Married partners should clearly see that the willful acceptance of temporary abstention has considerable spiritual, emotional and even physical merit. While total and heroic asceticism cannot be the common rule, or even the common ideal, some measure of the virtue of restraint is indispensable.

A valid solution to the difficulties of sex implies a clear understanding of the relative values of gratification and privation. Gratification is not the object of an absolute right, while privation is an inescapable condition of the imperfect state of man. Gratification is a privilege, a reward, an exceptional enchantment that colors the dreariness of life. We have no more right to its constant perfection than to perfect health or unlimited wealth. Let us then seek with care and patience – and treasure as a fragile and rare possession – whatever happens to be our share of happiness, realizing all the while that this share is dependent upon the quality of our offering, and limited by our imperfection and that of our partner.

Even at its best, sex could never be all satisfying, for in the most perfect marriage there is always a measure of hunger and pining, not only because we never receive as much as we would like, but also because we can give so little — and that, for the generous, is the deeper pain.

By their very nature, affective and erotic love are limited in many ways. They are limited in their all-too-human subject and object, in their material means of expression, in their lack of duration, and even in their intrinsic frailty, which can leave the lovers weeping when they come down from the summit of ecstasy. This indicates, not that such a summit is evil, but that it is far below a supreme and all-encompassing delight.

No pleasure short of the Beatific Vision may ever be taken as an absolute. No created pleasure can be anything but the aftermath of a deed well done. In order to be legitimate and virtuous, it must be enjoyed at the level of its imperfect existential value. Sexual pleasure is good and satisfying as an effect of orderly love, but endlessly disappointing when it is the bittersweet fruit of a tyrannical urge.

That is why there is no justification for those exalted lovers who seek in their relationship some kind of mystical delight. Such an ideal may seem admirable and moving in its literary expressions, but in real life anyone who seeks an absolute in sentimental or erotic love is chasing a chimera, for the all-satisfying and all-perfect pleasure of human love simply does not exist.

Now about pain. It is unrealistic again to deny or minimize the harmful effects of continence on those whose vocation is marriage. The simple truth is that total lack or severe limitation of sexual satisfaction often results in a state of nervous tension and unrest that has both physical and emotional effects. This pain cannot be disregarded, and yet it does not justify the search for compensations opposed to the moral law.

The argument that "everybody does it" and the waving of

the Kinsey report as a justification for sexual laxity would make sense only if the majority were naturally wise: their reaction to any given situation would then be generally right and sound. But since the fall, and because of concupiscence, the reaction of the masses is more often wrong and unhealthy. It is not in following the crowd that we will do right, but in standing by what we know to be better than what the crowd is seeking.

The problem of continence is very real for all, for the religious, for the lay celibates, and for the married, but it is different in each of these three cases. For the religious, the problem is solved in the sense of a definitive sublimation which clarifies the issue once and for all, not in a negative way, but in a manner that eliminates the possibility of physical fulfillment. For those who are preparing for marriage, it is a potential power, to be controlled in the present and used in the future. For the married, it is an actual power, to be controlled and used in the present. For the latter, the constant presence of the sexual partner makes of continence a question of existential import. There is no denying that it is a severe privation, at times even an excruciating sorrow.

Unfulfilled sexual love may produce bitter pain and desolation and give rise to a sense of utter loneliness, even despair. For what is sought is perfect and vital communication, and so very often what is had is very close to nothing. So brutal is the contrast that it may leave man or woman in a state of burning resentment or dull despondency. When all the physical mechanisms are in full functioning order, when every external influence contributes as it does in our modern world to an atmosphere of easy gratification, it is indeed cruel torture to remain with the deepest instinct unsatisfied. But since all things of man, the pleasurable and painful alike, may be lifted up to the level of the spirit, there is rich value in this very suffering. This is true for the married as well as for the unmarried, because there are in a truly dedicated marriage many more occasions for continence than for pleasure.

Two questions may be asked: Is such pain justified? Is it tolerable?

Either man is made for satisfaction in this life, and pain is then evil; or he is made for greater things, and pain may be a means toward them. The Christian position is crystal clear: man is made for the total happiness of the Beatific Vision, compared to which no pleasure is of any worth. The proper goal of human life is much higher than total and glorious sexual fulfillment: it is total and glorious search for the living God. To deny oneself some transitory joy, even at the cost of mental, nervous and physical pain, makes perfect sense as a genuine source of merit toward the acquiring of total joy. Within the framework of the greater task, however, the pleasure of sex may be accepted with gratitude, and the privation of it offered in a spirit of peaceful sacrifice. Suffering, then, may be endured by the power of what is higher in man, by the spirit which is superior to anything that afflicts him, because no suffering is too much when considered as a means toward the Perfect Love.

While there is a universal duty to alleviate suffering, we have no absolute right to a painless life. It is in this sense — of inescapable pain accepted willfully for the sake of moral truth — that the suffering of continence is justified. Since the purpose of life is not the elimination of pain but the acquisition of perfect joy, the pain required as a preliminary to this joy should be accepted joyfully.

Is the pain of continence tolerable? Besides the general theological principle that God provides grace and strength in proportion to our needs, there is also this: most of our pains are mental, and they are as severe as we make them. The pain of continence becomes intolerable when we make it so, when we attach so much importance to sexual pleasure that to be deprived of immediate gratification appears unendurable. That is, when we have so little control over our instincts that they become tyrannical; when we have perverted the order of human dignity by making the rational element a slave of the instinctual. The pain of continence is indeed intolerable if we build up sexual desire to the level of obsession; if we have so pampered our physiological system as to have lost control over its natural urges and to have surrendered to them as to a compulsive addiction.

There is little doubt about the tyranny of sex. Since the fall, sex has often assumed such immense proportions as to overwhelm the will and to bring about countless distortions in the lives of individuals, communities and societies. What needs to be overcome is not the sexual urge itself, which is a potent lever of action, life and love, but sexual dominance by which one limited power of man takes on excessive authority. Sex must be the servant of our wholeness and holiness, not the master of our dispersion and degradation. Besides the spiritual weapons of prayer and the sacraments, the best way to change it into a potent ally is precisely the practice of self-denial, or temporary continence and restraint, as opposed to unbridled self-indulgence. For tyranny thrives only when fostered by submissive slaves. Any act of willful freedom hampers its growth. Every time we fall into disorder, we become a little more strongly chained, a little more passively subject to vice. But every time we stand up in the freedom of our will and declare ourselves superior to our instincts, the shackles of bad habits are loosed, finally to fall to the ground.

What we need is not so much concentration on birth control as on sex control. What we need is a humanizing and rationalizing of the sexual relationship that would make it obey the commands of the mind and will within the context of charitable and sacrificial love. Even with the soothing effect of generous consent, the pain of continence will still be heavy, but it will no longer be intolerable, for it is exactly to this sacrificial pain that grace is proportioned: not to the torture of lust, but to the suffering brought about by unfulfilled desire for total physical union with the sacramental partner.

We are not alone in the world of earthly love, nor are we alone in the world of souls. We cannot remain indifferent at the sight of so many who, through ignorance or malice, abuse the gifts of God. The best we can do is to realize that we are part of the communion of saints, and offer our own sufferings and renunciations, hungers and privations, disappointments and sorrows in partial payment not only for our own debts but also for those of others. Let us consciously and willfully atone for the countless sexual sins, for broken homes and abandoned children, for abortions by the million, for the irresponsible rushing of adolescents into impossible unions, for the scandal of so many public figures gallivanting from divorce to divorce in their endless and fruitless search for happiness: endless, because they ignore the true meaning of life; fruitless, because they lack any fertile sense of love.

Personal discipline is a powerful antidote to all such disorder. And yet, the very notion of discipline seems as foreign to many as if it were a relic from the distant past. When emphasis is constantly placed on freedom of personal expression, discipline appears as a negative idea reminiscent of the Dark Ages, in complete contrast with the enlightened liberty of our progressive ways. Still, it is precisely in this, in the rational control over instinctive powers, that man rises above animality. As there must be refinement and measure in the use of food and drink, so there must be tenderness and control in the use of sex. And control in the matter of sex is much more important than measure in matters of food and drink, for abuse of the latter results in mere intoxication or indigestion, while the disorderly use of sex leads to personally destructive consequences.

The greater the effect of any power, the more discipline is needed for its proper use. There is in man no stronger physical urge than the desire to copulate. Throughout history, it has caused the most tragic crimes and the most poignant dramas, but also the highest forms of happiness — not to mention the fact that without it there would be no actors in the play of life.

Discipline, then, is a much-needed manly — and maidenly — virtue. It brings out the best in both sexes, for it is founded on mutual respect: respect of our own body and of that of the other in their most personal and intimate function.

Respect must not be confused with shame (*erubescentia*), since shame arises only out of guilt, and in spite of medieval pronouncements to the contrary, there is no intrinsic guilt in the act of love. The sex organs are worthy of respect in the sense of awe (*verenda, pudenda*) before the great mysteries of interpersonal communication and the reproduction of life.

In the disciplined acceptance of unfulfilled desire, there is a tremendous wealth which increases the pleasure of love, not only through avoidance of satiety and arousal of interest, but also through the impact of the sexual phenomena upon the man and wife who practice continence. The love of virtue coincides with the virtue of love – that is, with the power to love in every possible way, including the physical, in a manner that procures greater joy. By the very fact of perfecting and ordaining the principles of sexual love, every instance of its act is perfected and ordained, and consequently yields ever-increasing delight.

In other words, the most modern and sophisticated and intelligent and pleasurable way of making love consists in complying in full with the true principles of Christian morality, with the requirements of discipline and self-control, with the doctrine of the primacy of the spirit and the dynamic power of love. All of which makes of the properly perfected physiological relationship the most complete and satisfying expression of human love, the meritorious fulfillment of a God-created desire, a prayer in act, cosmic in dimension and personal in quality, an expression of total acquiescence – an Amen to the humanity of man redeemed by the divinity of Christ.

If, then, we approach the problems of sex with the firm purpose of making the most of what is human in it and avoiding what is not; with humble awareness that if we are left to our own weakness we will fall; but also with the certainty that with the help of grace anything can be done, with surprisingly little effort we will be able to preserve premarital chastity and to live a married life conformed to God's will. With surprisingly little effort, yes, but not without pain. Individual occasions and temptations will, with grace, be overcome promptly; however, grace removes neither the longing nor the solitude. God in his kindness knows that such sorrow and expectation, such waiting of a clean and hungering heart for the fulfillment of its dream of love will greatly increase the capacity for such love — and the gratitude of those lovers whose dream has come true.

In no other period of history has there been a better chance for the happy development of this dream of love. Many of the elements of sexual truth have been present for centuries, either fully revealed or able to be developed, albeit painfully, through research and experimentation. But it is only now that all the pieces of a truly human and satisfactory solution seem to be falling into place. The picture presents few blanks to the observing mind. As soon as a reasonable solution is found and approved concerning the regulation of fertility, and continence is turned from an intolerable imposition into a willful sacrifice, then there will be a real chance for a golden age of married love. Husband and wife will then be free to determine, in the light of their conscience, the number of children they wish to have; they will conceive them purposefully and joyfully, adding to the natural pleasure of their love the formal desire to make it procreative. In those intervals in which pregnancy is undesirable, and after fulfilling their family plan, they will be free to lavish on each other the full measure of their sexual gift without the constant poison of calculation and fear.

What so many good people are hoping for is not sexual license, but so complete a "hominization" of sex that it may become fully dependent in both its purposes upon a free and rational choice, instead of being hampered as it is now by the anguish of producing unwanted life. Children will be born according to reason, each one willed and welcome; and husband and wife will be for each other a means of happiness, grace and peace instead of the instruments of torture they so often happen to be in the present state of affairs.

Much more confidence and freedom should be given to the

individual conscience. No act of blind obedience will ever have the meritorious value of the free choice dictated by an enlightened and personalistic love of God. This will be seen to be particularly true regarding the question of birth control. Any practical solution imposed by the Church will be immensely more damaging than a determination of principles and a recognition of the freedom of conscience of individual couples.

Part Two

THE FLOWERING OF SEX

XI

Preparation for Marriage

"Faith shall be blest we know not how
And love fulfilled we know not where."
COVENTRY PATMORE

In an agricultural society or in one of artisans, economic independence coincides with sexual maturity, since both depend upon physical development. In such societies, young people can make a living at the very time they are ready for marriage. In our technological world, on the contrary, the time lag between sexual maturity and possible marriage is being stretched at both ends. Intense provocation and the bad habit of early dating advance the age of awakening, while the necessities of education and training for complicated jobs postpone both economic independence and sexual satisfaction in marriage.

For those strongly called to marriage, total continence over a long period of time is not nearly as harmless as we are often made to believe. There is a constant buildup of anguish, nervous tension and physical frustration that may result in headaches, depression and irritability. One young man brought up "in the best Catholic tradition" who was suffering from these symptoms believed .they were due to some organic disease or deficiency. He consulted a Parisian doctor of high repute — and was very much upset and scandalized when told the simple truth: that the only thing he needed was a girl.

137

Man is so much made for woman and woman for man that, except in the case of a clear vocation to the religious life, continence is achieved only at the cost of severe and painful repression. Continued over too long a period, it sets up serious obstacles to the happy and natural relation between the sexes, and may even lead to atrophy of the psychic mechanism of pleasure. Full compliance with the moral laws of sex in the prevailing atmosphere of laxity makes of the chaste young man something of an outcast. He is no longer "with it." He suffers in his body, emotions and mind. His marriage may be damaged by the very fact of his uncompromising respect for sex and woman. This is not a pessimistic view but the plain, factual truth. It is a real problem, but what can be done about it?

Little can be done about the overwhelming emphasis on sex in popular literature, advertising and show business. Some results could be gained from a concentrated effort to tone down the importance and social imperative of early dating. Nothing at all will ever again decrease the length of the training period in preparation for life in the modern world.

Separation of the sexes in schools and universities seems ineffective as a means for the preservation of sexual integrity. In most cases, compensations are sought as soon as freedom replaces restraint. Furthermore, the lack of mutual recognition and daily contact marks the relation between the sexes with a dangerous unreality which often results in a poor choice of partner. Coeducation, then, in spite of the risk of early dating, seems to provide the better preparation for life. Our society must be faced as it is and its tensions solved objectively.

Two ways are open. The one says, "Remorse is better than regret." The other, "Regret is better than remorse." The first is the way of the pragmatic hedonist, living entirely for the here and now, cultivating his sexual instinct and indulging in sexual gratification before marriage, in opposition to the moral law. He is legion, and so long as he can manage not to think

— that is, not to act as a rational human being — he may show the appearance of happiness and the glow of health. Not only is this way in complete contradiction with the Commandments and Gospels: it is precisely those unions marked with antecedent lack of control which end up most often on the rocks.

In the second way, that of chastity, most of the natural joys of early manhood are inevitably sacrificed for the sake of something greater and better: the full stature of the child of God who places the realities of revealed truth above the clamor of instinctive desire.

The first is the common way, the second that of heroic sanctity. Can we expect it to be followed? It is the only alternative to fornication — an ugly word representing an ugly thing: sex, not necessarily without love, but without that total personal involvement which makes it sacred. In teaching premarital chastity, traditional moralists are fully right. But they should realize that what is frustrated is not mere greed or lust, but the very perfection of man, the desire to give and to love. They should see how much it implies physical and moral torture — and possible damage — all of which is justified only because man is made for greater things than perfect sexual fulfillment.

Some contact between boy and girl is necessary, however, during the period of enforced waiting. Even in the absence of any immediate prospect of marriage, there must be some testing of compatibilities, some emotional expression of sex, within the boundaries of tenderness, devotion and mutual respect. The main problem, of course, is to determine the limits of permissible intimacies. In general, this must be left to the individual conscience. The choice is always difficult and involves some risk: sexual contacts, even the lightest, such as holding hands, follow a pattern of increasing hunger and compulsion, each permissive step preparing for the next until the urge becomes almost uncontrollable. When a fire is started, no one really knows how far it will spread. Between permissible intimacies and a raging conflagration of the senses, the margin is dangerously thin because it is made up of a succession of almost imperceptible steps.

There is, however, in every conscience a very clear and persistent voice which indicates where to stop. The exact limit may vary according to experience, temperament, or refinement of the moral sense, but the voice is always there, and it must be heeded under pain of losing control. As long as marriage is impossible, it is of the utmost importance not to indulge in what may in one partner be within the range of discipline, but could lead the other into excessive emotional or physical cravings the violence of which may then throw the couple off balance. The limits of indulgence, then, must depend not only on one's own capacity, but also on the maturity of the other.

In each case, the problem must be solved in the light of the general principles outlined above; that is, in the light of the total man and woman, of their natural and supernatural ends — and with the constant awareness that sexual fulfillment is not an absolute right, and that some measure of suffering and restraint is a necessary prelude to pleasure, even on the natural level.

Adolescents realize, clearly or confusedly according to the level of their education, that they lack full understanding and wisdom; they are often afraid of their own freedom and power, and rarely do they resent the strong hand that directs them with prudence and justice. In spite of the natural rebelliousness of youth, they prefer to be "told" than to be left alone. But the "telling" must be the communication of one rational being with another, and not the command of a misinformed autocrat.

Young people are both highly interested and vaguely scared by their developing sensual powers. In spite of much bragging and assertion of self, they know only too well that they do not have all the answers. If their natural idealism and dignity are challenged and cultivated, these virtues will flower into married love. But they must be challenged most clearly and cultivated systematically.

Much blame rests on parents for letting go, for allowing their children to take every possible liberty in the name of a false right "to develop their personalities." Under such circumstances, development is confined to the disorders due to original sin. What is needed from childhood on is the clear notion that discipline is a condition of happiness, that it consists in the proper use of freedom. There is a great difference between a liberal and a licentious education. The contemporary trend is too often toward the latter.

Once again, in this matter, all depends upon personal circumstances and the degree of moral refinement attained by individuals. Some may rise to an ideal of heroic purity, abstaining even from the slightest sexual contact. This may be wrong if based on timidity or a sense of guilt. But it may also be a magnificent preparation for the highest gift, for the gift of all and everything to the one and true mate. It may be the attitude of the poltroon or of the saint.

I am not saying that some measure of sensual expressivity cannot be combined with purity: it certainly can, when it corresponds to true love and is maintained within the limits of prudence. I am simply indicating the highest ideal of chastity, which may appear to some as a lack of manliness or femininity, when in fact it is a summit of moral refinement.

Traditional moralists are right in endorsing premarital chastity but, as we have seen, they are often wrong in their teachings concerning the fulfillment of marriage. Instead of seeing in the sexual relationship the highest expression of union as willed by God, they too often consider it as a hindrance to the spiritual life, a loss of innocence, a thing to be spurned, toned down, reduced to a minimum. It has been my thesis all along that the opposite is true: that the sexual relationship in its fullest development is an occasion of increase in the spiritual life through the flowering of happiness and the growth of

gratitude; an acquiring of new innocence, that of total involvement in the providential plan; a thing to be exalted, increased,
lifted up to a maximum of human dignity and delight. Only
then will the wounds of early sacrifices be healed in the fire
of love.

True love begins as a quest for a treasure. It cannot be left
to the caprice of the wind: it must be willful and persevering,
prayerful and humble. The first step consists in kneeling in the
solitude of each one's unique and personal self and praying to
God for enlightenment as to what he expects. The answer will
not come readymade as from a computer. But the importance
of such prayer lies in having made the act of offering in a mood
of availability and goodwill, in having made ourselves sensitive to the impulses of the Spirit.

If, after such an act of submission to God's will, it becomes
increasingly clear that marriage is our true vocation, the next
question is the choice of a partner.

Both man and woman always seek a mate who is as close to
their idea of perfection as their own imperfection permits. But
since man and woman, although rational, are free to abuse
their reason, this "best" which is always sought is not always
true and objective perfection: it may very well be some image
distorted by ignorance, misunderstanding, prejudice or sin.
There is a first obligation, then, to straighten out our ideas
about marriage itself and the nature of the ideal partner.

There may also be the danger of aiming too high, for then
the realities of life will never come close enough to our dream.
In fact, what often happens is that we have to bring down
our fairyland idol peg by peg until it matches a true and living
person. Maturity in this respect consists in the ability to appre-
ciate the other, not as an extension of our imagination, but as
a distinct person.

For the Christian, there is a redeeming factor to human
imperfection: when in marriage we witness the marvel of a
free and unique and loving individual of the opposite sex willing to bind his or her destiny unconditionally and unreservedly

to our own, such a gift properly understood overcomes the frailties of fallen nature and brings the partners up again, peg by peg, to the perfection of enjoying God together throughout eternity.

A word, now, on a characteristic phenomenon of early love which I will call "fixation."

It seems that, with few exceptions, young men and women concentrate the sum total of their attention and desires upon a single individual of the opposite sex. This may be taken as a natural sign of the monogamous requirement of true marriage. Ideally, and in conformity with moral law, such fixation refers to a suitable mate and endures throughout married life. In fact, however, it often refers to a completely unsuitable person, or skips from one to another with a suddenness and irrationality comparable only to the suddenness and irrationality of the original adventure. The former idol, then, falls with such completeness that the appeal vanishes, and the fickle lover is left to wonder what on earth could have produced the soul-shattering desire of perhaps no more than a few weeks before.

The same phenomenon appears at all ages, but more often in young lovers. The reason is that youthful ardor and immaturity add their pull to the irrational instinctual drive. Quite often, then, with the very young, a fixation is but the result of the love of love. It consists in attributing to a chosen person all the characteristics of ideal love. The young lover is kept in a state of Platonic adoration that feeds his or her emotional needs even in the absence of physical satisfaction. But the state itself is far from ideal, for it results in much tension and repression and may be nervously upsetting. Yet it is considerably less damaging than premarital experimenting, for it preserves personal integrity, and its hardships may be accepted in a spirit of sacrifice in anticipation of the glories of true and complete love.

At the time when marriage is possible, fixation is good when it applies to a suitable partner, but it may be quite damaging if it does not. If it is unilateral and combined with a false sense of duty and faithfulness, it may drag out a one-sided engagement for years, leading to nothing but a tragic vacuum or ending up in a disastrous marriage. In a true marriage, each partner looks up to the other; in one that results from late and reluctant consent to a one-sided fixation, one partner will always look up and the other down, and the fundamental balance will be upset from the start.

It is infinitely better to make a clean break of such an engagement, pre-engagement, or promise made to oneself than to run the risk of being chained for life to the wrong mate. This may hurt at first and require some measure of stoic readjustment. Some ancient wounds of love may never really heal, and yet old loves may be replaced surprisingly soon with new, more vital and dynamic adventures. This is one case when the rapid rate of transfer of love-fixation is truly advantageous.

As an extreme case of dangerous fixation, there is the "sacrificial" marriage — which entails no heroic virtue, but only monumental presumption and imprudence. The sacrificial marriage is that in which one partner, without the slightest obligation to do so, has chosen a mate whom he or she hopes to redeem from some vice or imperfection. What is wrong is the fact of the actual vice or imperfection being the clincher, the reason why marriage has been sought, for there is here a kind of masochism, a self-imposed martyrdom that is much more stupid than meritorious. The norms of Christian charity impose no obligation whatsoever of risking one's whole marital life on such a gamble as some expected change in personality supposedly to be brought about by the "heroic" partner. This, of course, is quite different from a marriage entered upon from motives of true love, and in which the partners help each other to overcome their weaknesses, for in such cases the basis of marriage is sound love, and not foolish self-sacrifice.

Let us now try to analyze the overwhelming compulsion which goes hand in hand with love-fixation. It often arises out of the blue. A companion, who for years had been nothing

more than just that, suddenly becomes IT, by what appears
as an inner revelation. The same may also happen suddenly
with a total stranger. The fixation acquires much of its strength
precisely because of the total irrationality of the magic shock.
Since it is irrationally produced, it violently resists rational
efforts to extinguish it; it fights for its life against time and
tide with quixotic and pitiful constancy. The fixation is quite
impervious to statistical arguments tending to prove that the
encounter with one person out of a narrow group has very
little chance of producing the ideal partner, and that there are
probably within reasonable distance several thousand others
who would do a better job.

The notion of the ideal mate is automatically associated with
the prejudice of fate, or destiny, or whatever you wish to call it.
Some marriages do seem to have been made in heaven, but the
usual procedure of heaven is to shower its graces upon those
unions which are established on a solid earthly foundation of
rational forethought and common sense; those in which fan-
tastic dreams have not been permitted to run wild, but in
which the choice has been conditioned and controlled by an
objective appraisal that is only possible in the preliminary
stages of love.

The foremost task of those who prepare for marriage is to
think out thoroughly what they want. In the absence of spiritual and rational forethought, fixation will go to work uncon-
trolled, or be set in motion by some quite unessential feature
— a mannerism, a tone of voice, a well-balanced gait, the slant
of an eye — that suffices to set ablaze the accumulated longing
for sexual union. If, on the other hand, sufficient thought has
been given in advance to the splendor and challenge of married
life, the choice of a partner will depend upon the presence in
him or her of the elements required for such life. And if over
and above these essential conditions — faith in the living God
of Love, a spirit of total dedication, full mutual confidence,
dynamic and active spirituality and so forth — there are offered
youth and beauty and charm and the promise of sexual enchant-

ment, all the better. Such things are good and they will mightily contribute to happiness. But love unprepared, unpremeditated and unprayed-for will catch fire on incidents alone and very likely end up in a divorce court.

In one of the preparatory reports to the Second Vatican Council, it was justly and seriously suggested that, since a period of novitiate is required before acceptance in a religious Order, and the possession of some specific, religious information is demanded before the reception of the sacraments of the Eucharist and Confirmation, something similar be demanded before marriage. This would introduce into the disciplinary regulations of the Church some sort of obligation for the engaged couple to attend preparatory sessions organized by competent authorities, and to prove their readiness for lifelong union. The practical form of such instruction could follow the lines of the Cana Conferences. This would certainly increase the chances of success.

Every marriage, in a sense, is a frightful gamble, and the possibilities of harmonious mating are slim indeed in any but a very primitive society. How can any man, who hardly knows himself, have the wisdom and insight to choose a wife with whom he can live in harmony during a lifetime of the most absolute intimacy? There may be few greater horrors than having to share not only one's house but even one's bed with a person whose manners are annoying. Many a marriage is wrecked by such idiosyncrasies.

With what levity do many enter into a partnership that must last until death! Think of the lonely grasping the last straw, engaging their whole life on not much more than the fact that the other belongs to the opposite sex; think of the shotgun marriages of children whose puppy love has been inflamed by premature dating and petting, generally through the fault of their parents; think of the greedy who seek in marriage nothing but the satisfaction of their lust; remember even the countless number of those who seemed to have a chance, and yet, through haste or lack of sound judgment, fall headlong into marriages that turn out to be complete failures.

Yes, indeed, marriage is a gamble. But does it have to be? From a purely natural viewpoint, there is no safe road to happiness, for marriage is the union of two free individuals whose freedom makes them liable at any time to break the tethers of convention and morality. But the world is not ruled by nature alone: above nature, there is the safe and mighty hand of God, all powerful and yet respectful of human freedom. In the choice of a partner, then, we should not despair, but trust in God, while taking every reasonable precaution. As the Arabs put it, "Trust in God — but tie the camel's leg!"

A successful married life depends much more on internal than on external circumstances. It is what a man or woman are in the freedom of their spirit which determines the tone of their intimate relationship. In that sense, there is a close connection between salvation and happiness in marriage, for both depend much more on what we do with what we have received than on the extent and quality of our natural gifts. A saint does not need to be a genius, nor does he need to be handsome, popular or witty: he needs merely to be what he is, in the light of his personal vocation. The same applies to the married: they have no essential need of outstanding intelligence, stunning beauty or engaging cleverness. It will suffice for them to be themselves, for every person is a deserving object of faithful love. The fact that Christ died for our salvation should be proof enough of the value of every man and woman. If they are of such great worth, Christian spouses who truly love each other may always find in each other enough nourishing value to sustain them for life.

That is why the fundamental motive of a marriage is so important. Any union built on a nonessential character will be dependent upon the continuance of the same character and will be wrecked by its disappearance. It may even be wrecked much sooner, as soon, in fact, as the nonessentiality of the character becomes evident. Many a man who married for money, physical beauty, a certain grace in manner, or promising sexual attributes has lived to regret his choice.

If more attention were given to education in matters of marriage, there would be less need for marriage clinics, with their pitiful attempts to patch up broken homes.

An adequate preparation for marriage consists first of all in the example of harmony between the parents. There are statistics to show the effect of bickering or separated parents upon the marital lives of their children. Hidden resentment, guilt complexes, anxieties before the challenges of life are but a few of these detrimental effects. All this adds greatly to the inherent risk of marriage itself.

Marriage is an art, for it is in the order of doing and it is only as good as we make it. As every art, it must be learned and perfected long before it is entered upon. The art of love is learned from loving parents, from daily and progressive efforts toward unselfishness, from an education that should truly be what the word implies: a drawing out of the best powers of the child, an ordering of desires in terms of relative value, a first rational step in the formation of a delicately balanced and self-determining conscience — and not what it is so often in fact: an indoctrination of Kantian imperatives, a memorization of facts that leaves the child bewildered in a world of events mostly dynamic and unforeseen. . . . But this is another story.

Proper sex education begins with infancy, not in the form of blind and stern taboos, but through kindly promptings and counsels geared to the individual's stage of development. These should not be part of a separate world, but of the general pattern of education, for laxity in matters of work, dress or other forms of behavior will make it impossible to obtain discipline in this one field. A child brought up in a haphazard and lackadaisical way will develop no more order and respect in its sexual habits than in anything else. On the contrary, because of the very power of sexual impulses, it is here that disorder will be the worst as soon as freedom becomes possible.

Sex education, then, should be part of the general training in self-control. Much has been written on the subject, and there is no need here to go into great detail. The conclusion of most works inspired by the true Christian spirit is that sexual education must be provided by the parents, in simple and direct words free of the promptings of guilt complexes and exactly adapted to the level of the question and of the questioner. There is no need, for instance, to provide a complete explanation of intercourse the first time a child asks where babies come from. A story will illustrate this point: One little girl asked her mother: "Mommy, where did I come from? Johnny told me in school where *he* came from!" The anxious mother, remembering her child-guidance pamphlets, began to explain about the birds and the bees and the cozy nest under mommy's heart. "Gee, Mom," said the little girl, "Johnny only came from Brooklyn!"

Respect must be taught very early, as soon as reason develops and long before any sign of puberty: respect for life and living things, respect for nature, and most of all respect for persons. Respect, also, for sex must be shown in the avoidance of low-level jokes on married life and, more positively, in proper attention to the specific obligations and qualities of man and woman. Once respect and discipline have begun to grow together, chastity, far from being impossible even in a sex-ridden world, becomes the natural thing. For, with a proper understanding of the value and sacredness of marriage, every premature indulgence will be taken for what it truly is: a shoddy substitute which will result only in spoiling the real thing. All the pragmatic talk about the advisability of premarital experience produces the most unpragmatic result that the glory and delight of a truly chaste marriage — in the positive sense of a feast of mutual discovery — are replaced by the blasé attitude of the couple for which all this is old stuff. Many young people of our time would be quite impervious to the higher spiritual reasons in defense of premarital chastity, but even pagans would respond to the argument that premarital sex spoils the fun. For the youth-in-the-street, the sexual relationship seems to be taken so much for granted, so matter-of-factly, that one is led to wonder how much of the delight of sex remains in the honeymoon trip. After an adolescence of petting and indulgence, the average young man selects a mate, and the same petting and indulgence continue with the blessing of Society. Can we really call "civilized" a way of life in which love has been reduced to this?

It is the very obstacles opposed to immediate gratification that maintain desire at its highest peak and offer pleasures of the greatest depth. If a young man or woman finds easy satisfaction at the outset of sexual development, the whole relationship so readily obtained may appear to be of little value. Early indulgence spoils the psychic buildup of expectation and destroys the magic and mystery of the opposite sex, which develop slowly and mature only as the fruits of ascetical restraint. Not that it is good to marry late, but that it is *not* good to marry before a period of thorough testing in self-control. When the sexual urge is satisfied as soon as it arises — and more so if this is done in casual matings of teen-agers with no intention of marriage — the sanctity, the sacredness, the wholeness of the gift of person to person never reaches the level of consciousness, of an intended good.

Chastity must be enforced by some measure of external discipline, by parents and school authorities, because the attractions of sex, increased by social laxity, are often beyond the means of control available to youth. There is a complete disparity between the natural urge, the constant temptation, the widespread example on the one hand, and the weakness of the untrained will on the other. Young people need to be protected against themselves for the sake of their later and greater happiness. The current happy-go-lucky, try-everything-once attitude is in complete contrast with the gravity of irreversible acts.

It is always the forbidden fruit that has the greatest appeal, so let us show that the fruit of sex is by no means forbidden — that on the contrary it is good and holy, worthy of expectation and eager desire. Restraint in matters of sex is not like taking candy away from a child, but like taking green fruit away because it is not yet ripe.

Young people should be told, not to extinguish their sex life, but to develop it by deepening its significance, by cultivating in themselves the proper notions of respect and generosity, and by becoming true persons capable of personal commitments and relationships. What chance of sexual fulfillment is there in lovemaking prompted by defiance of authority and resulting in clumsy attempts during premature dating? This is not good enough. There is much more to sex: there is something much warmer, much more human and complete, much more solid and satisfying, and also much more erotically pleasurable. It is no use saying, "Shame on you! Don't do this, or don't do that!" What should be said is, "Go all the way, delightfully and joyfully, but not before the time is right; not before you are able to give in full the person that you are; not before you have found the mate who can answer with a corresponding gift."

Chivalrous devotion to some fair lady appears as a much healthier introduction to marriage than any immature indulgence in sex. Unhappy is the man whose early years were not enlightened by ecstasy at the thought or in the presence of the beloved! There is in such love a quality of dedication that is innocent of any selfishness. "The first love is not the only love, but it is often the only one into which self does not enter": [1] it is entirely outgoing and altruistic. Self, in fact, is so entirely absent from the whole process, and the level of love is so idealistically high, that the damsel so youthfully wooed is often disappointed not to recognize in herself the glorified being she has become in the young lover's eyes. What he loves is not a living woman; what he offers is not a living man. What he loves is his own concept of the perfection of love, and what he offers is his burning heart. And what can

[1] Hugh Walpole, *The Young Enchanted.*

a young lady do with such a heart, except perhaps bask in its sunshine? The young lover cannot give anything more; he cannot give himself because he does not as yet possess himself. His notion of love is too lofty to be integrated with his person. And yet, again, unhappy the young man who has never soared to these heights of longing, for they contain one important element of love: the tendency to perfection.

What, then, is a proper preparation for marriage? It consists in reading the right kind of books, speaking to the right kind of counselors, and producing within the mind the right kind of picture, both real and ideal, of what marriage truly is. Let those who have not received such counseling go after it and seek it from the wise and experienced well in advance of the time when a choice will have to be made. It is then that the proper child/parent relationship is so important. Provided they are sufficiently wise and aware of their children's needs, parents are by nature and vocation, and also by their grace of state, the very best counselors in these vital matters. Let young people, then, set a few clear and absolute conditions to their choice, and wait in peace with open eyes and an open heart, trusting in the one who said, "It is not good for man to be alone." As long as we ask nothing but the will of God, that will shall be accomplished in us, and the will of God is that mankind increase and multiply.

Even if hopeful lovers remain alone for a long time, there is no need for revolt or bitterness. It may be that God is reserving for them a great gift, awaiting their greater maturity, increasing their capacity for love in order to give them more than their heart could have contained when it was too young. *And even if this expectation lasts until death, they will have expected perfectly the love of that Lover who always comes.*

XII

What Sex Is Not

"Where is the life we have lost in living?"
T. S. ELIOT

Important as it is, *sex is not an end in itself* — and much less is it a career. Even aside from the viewpoint of morality, a Don Juan or ladies' man is one with a totally distorted sense of proportion who suffers from an inferiority complex which he attempts to overcome through constant self-assertion. Such a man is not a powerful hero, but a pitiful weakling in spite of any amount of operatic emotion that may surround his succession of failures.

Love in all its forms has essentially a single object. Any scattering is a sure sign of imperfection and abuse. Its name, then, becomes legion. True love seeks no fame, nor does it gloat over its victories. It is much too deep and personal to tolerate publicity, and much too good and satisfying to bear comparison with anything else. A man who claims there are better things on earth than to spend a night with his wife is not truly married to her — and he deserves both pity and blame, for either he or his wife, or both, have failed in the art of love.

Sex is not merely a hygienic habit. At the bottom level of the literary scale, sex is made to be little more than a form of physical relief. There is need, of course, to remove all exag-

153

gerated glamor from physical love, but not to the extent of taking away what makes of it much more than an animal function: the personal quality of the gift mutually offered and accepted by husband and wife. The expression "sexual outlet," which recurs throughout the Kinsey reports, suggests that, in the minds of the investigators, sex was considered merely as a fact of physiological life. The whole study consists in a cold statistical survey of how sexual pressure is generally relieved. It is a factual study, but the approach is more frightening in its scientific materialism than is the mass of immorality so blatantly revealed. If these statistics are to be taken as representative of average morality — and not as only expressing the opinion of those few people of loose conscience who were willing to speak freely of their sexual disorders — two clear conclusions may be drawn: an almost complete lack of self-control and moral sense among the average population; and, as a natural corollary, an almost general loss and misunderstanding of the true glories of sex.

Sex is not a hopeless illusion. There is no particular virtue, and there may be much ignorance and even ingratitude, in the so-frequent expressions of defeatism in matters of sex. True resignation is the graceful acceptance of some unavoidable pain. This is a far cry from giving up all hope of sexual fulfillment after a few blundering attempts in early life. Such false resignation goes hand in hand with the notion that sex is overrated; that its marvels exist only in the poet's mind; that they come true only in the lives of some lucky few who receive them as a special gift from the gods. To the frustrated, accounts of the prowesses of love appear either as deeds of unholy passion, or as fantasies with as little reality as the exploits of Jason and the Argonauts.

To be sure, there are degrees in the ability to love and to be loved, but such degrees are generally a matter of culture and intentional effort. Sexual love developing from true personal qualities properly nourished and made to bloom is neither wicked nor illusory: it is as healthy and real as apple pie, and immensely satisfying because it both challenges and appeases the whole man and woman. It is the privilege, not of a few, but of all those called to the married state who approach it with a clean and generous heart.

When life in the bedroom — or, according to taste, in the framework of sunny beach or shady forest — loses its salt, it is often because the nature and function of sex have been misunderstood. Every couple needs both preliminary knowledge and sustained research in the art of love, a constantly cultivated understanding that sex is a limited but marvelously rich and perfectible aspect of the human complex, spiritual, emotional and material.

Sex is not a right, in the sense that one partner in marriage may demand satisfaction from the other at any time. The heavy-handed notion of a man's "marriage rights" is gross enough to kill any chance of sexual harmony. It takes two to make love, and both must be willing and active. Many a possessive male seems to have overlooked at his own expense the wisdom of Ecclesiastes: "For everything, there is a season, and a time for every matter under heaven: a time to embrace, and a time to refrain from embracing . . ." (3:1,5). Perhaps the time to refrain is the more fruitful, for as ". . . sorrows come to stretch out spaces in the heart for joy" (Edwin Markham), restraint stretches out spaces in the heart for pleasure. Instead of routine and satiety, there is the powerful buildup of anticipation and expectation. And there is also this: in giving pleasure to a woman at her own time, there is much greater delight than in seeking it from her as one pleases.

Sex is not absolute bliss, as it would appear to the reader of pulp magazines. The story generally runs as follows: Boy meets girl and falls in love (*i.e.*, believes he could not survive without instant copulation); something comes up to hold them apart; obstacle is removed, and they make love in a state of delirious happiness forever after.

These are but fairy tales for the consolation of the frustrated, but they are harmful in that they convey an utterly erroneous

idea of physical love by presenting it as an adequate means
of perfect and eternal pleasure. In fact, when two incompletely
prepared young people enter the state of matrimony, bitter
disillusion may be the first thing to strike, even before the
honeymoon is over, for marriage is not all "taking" and having
fun. There is a lot more to it, and most of it is "giving." Every
true marriage consists in a certain loss of freedom, concentration of scattered emotions upon the one chosen partner, and
the burden of providing for the domestic society. Such things
are painful for those whose former life consisted in unrestricted
liberty, and who saw in marriage nothing more than the legal-
izing of their pleasure.

Sex is not a constant erotic orgy. The state of marriage is
but one of the possibilities of human life, the most frequently
sought. It has its proper pleasures and pains, its moments of
exaltation and depression, its periods of growth and decay,
of exuberant health and weakening sickness. The perfect flowering of physical love demands the highest state of readiness in
both lover and beloved. Complete gratification, then, can
neither be taken for granted nor furiously sought. Whenever it
is not obtainable, there is no reason to wail to the high heavens
that we have been robbed. The too-ardent pursuit of perfect
satisfaction where there is at best but frail and passing joy
will lead to such tenseness and greed that the true flower of
passion may never come to bloom.

For a married couple living in spirit and in truth, some of
the most simple and natural joys of life may be almost beyond
reach. What the pagan and the hedonist gather by the handful
may be a rare and cherished privilege for those who live the
Beatitudes — but it will have immensely greater value and
procure immensely deeper satisfaction for the latter.

Sex is not automatic pleasure. A wife should not be expected
to perform as a trained seal every time the proper signal is
given. She should be left entirely free to her own mood and
rhythm. The most perfect encounters are those of two freedoms, so deeply respectful of each other that there is no

demand on either side, but a mutual desire and a mutual offering of the means of joy. A man, however, does not always have to wait for positive signs: he can very well take the initiative, patiently and lovingly, in the hope of awakening Sleeping Beauty, but it should be in a spirit of expectation, not of greed. If nothing happens, or very little, so be it. He will receive his pleasure in full some other time if he can hold his peace.

Sex, finally, is not organized delight. The greatest moments of love are never planned: they simply come — yet never to the unprepared. The best attitude is one of eager and kind attention and availability; a state of presence, of awareness of the partner's need and mood, free from any systematic charting. Love is not made by appointment: it must rise from a sudden glory that too much hunger or concern may kill. But, when the moment comes, finding bride and spouse in a sweet and holy exaltation, such is their joy that a single successful experience may suffice to enlighten a whole lifetime with its happy memory.

ꙮ XIII

The Natural Goodness of Sex

> "The appreciation of the sensual is the mark of
> human rationality and not of animal instinct."
>
> ERIC GILL

All of us should fight the prejudice of shame and darkness that
is still casting its shadow on sexual things in general, and particularly on woman considered as their instrument. All of us
should approach these matters with a mind both open and
clean, yet constantly aware of human frailty and of the gaping
pits of possible disorder.

Let us realize once and for all that God made sex, and made
it good. Nowhere in the Bible is it said or implied that the
physical union of man and wife is sinful or wicked as such, or
that it has been irretrievably vitiated. The powers of sex were'
created for a purpose which was good at the origin and
remained good after the fall. God, furthermore, could not have
created sex without providing the means for its proper use.

As seen in the perspective of the whole man, sex may be
defined as the complex pattern of differences existing between
man and woman, leading to the desire for that community of
life which results in sacramental, sentimental and physical
intimacy and finds its fruit in the child. Sex is good, clean,
natural and wholesome in its act and in all of its most vital
and passionate expressions. It is challenging, stimulating, vivi-

silent conversation: "I know, and you know, and I am grateful for the wonder of it."

Sex is with us to stay. We can no more erase it from our minds than eliminate it from our bodies. Nor is there the slightest reason to do so, particularly when its expressions are a specific element of our sacramental state of life. There is so much fun and excitement in the sweet complicity of shared secrets, in the memory of past intimacies and the anticipation of further experiences that to deny oneself a generous portion of sexual daydreaming — the dread *delectatio morosa* of the Scholastic — amounts to an excessive limitation of the bond between husband and wife.

One of the most delicate matters in the management of sex as a natural good is the drawing of a reasonable line between indulgence and restraint. That both extremes are wrong is easy to see: the prude is as ridiculous as the libertine. But where, exactly, is the perfect level of sexual balance? When will the intimate life of a married couple be both rich and virtuous?

A rich sexual life is in no way incompatible with the highest virtue. This will be developed later when we come to the Virtue of Sex.

In a matter so much dependent upon passionately prejudiced and emotionally subjective opinions, it may seem difficult to find a common standard. Our task is made more difficult by the fact that every normal couple believes its own experience to be unique. The manifestations of sex, however, like those of any other human activity, are part of a stable and constant element in man which philosophy calls the human essence, and which we have seen in earlier chapters to be the foundation of sexual morality.

The right attitude toward sex is objective, reasonable, and free from obsession. It is objective when it takes into account the all-too-real limitations of the sexual relationship, even at its best. It is reasonable when, instead of falling into an irrational and childish revolt every time delight proves impossible, the lovers conform to whatever is at hand and do not pine for what is out of reach. It is free from obsession when they consider satisfaction, not as the foremost goal of their life, but as the crowning of their togetherness, the limited and yet enchanting expression of totally dedicated love.

A married saint accepts sex simply and gracefully as one of the means by which glory may be rendered to God, and he ordains his sexual life in function of that glory. Such ordering applies to the selection of a partner, to a charitable relationship between the spouses, and also to a lavish mutual gift of every legitimate pleasure. Pure and ideal marriage does not consist in living as brother and sister. Such is perfect for brother and sister and for the unmarried. But there is something completely forced, unnatural and contradictory in the notion that the perfection of marriage consists in permanent renunciation of its fundamental act. Since intercourse, as any other natural act, is not evil as such but morally indifferent and may become a true moral good when properly performed, there sometimes may be greater virtue in making love than in abstaining from it. A truly perfect and pure marriage is one in which every act, including the most vital and intimate, is motivated and brought to full glory by true love.

In some exceptional cases the practice of absolute continence is demanded of a married couple. This, however, is motivated and justified, not by the desire to make marriage more perfect, but by reasons entirely extrinsic to the matrimonial union. Such a marriage does not become a better marriage because of its renunciation of physical intimacies: it may, however, become a better state of life through a calling entirely foreign to marriage.

Within a perfect and pure marriage, there can be a true virtue of sensuality. Sensuality may be defined as the capacity of drawing pleasure from the experience of the senses, from a beautiful sight, a charming sound, a stirring fragrance, a provocative touch, an exciting taste. It is the direct and natural effect of the meeting of sensitive organs with their proper object. These organs are part of man as God created him. Their response to environment is automatic, but the use made of this response and the manner in which it is sought are dependent upon the laws of morality for, as already noted, a pleasure is good only when it is the effect of an act which is itself good.

The virtue of sensuality, then, consists in the proper use of pleasure. No man can survive without a certain amount of sensorial challenge and response to it, and every response to a well-proportioned challenge brings forth pleasure. This can be avoided only by preventing any contact of the senses with their proper object. Total prevention leads to death, and prolonged privation to insensitivity through atrophy of the organs. This, in turn, is an impairment of the human complex.

Since apart from mystical revelation nothing comes to the intellect except through the senses, and everything that comes through the senses results either in pleasure or pain, to deprive oneself of the wealth of sensory experience may be so total an impoverishment as to leave the mind with no other resource than to feed on itself, to be caught in a maze of sterile deductive constructions, to spin in a squirrel cage of prejudices due to the refusal to see the world as it is — a common phenomenon in medieval writings and in the works of those who preserve the Gothic state of mind.

What is wrong with sensuality is not that it may be pleasurable but that it may be sought as an absolute end. The ancients had a word for this, *frui*, which means to enjoy something unqualifiedly, as a supreme good. It is in that sense that sensuality is irrational and subhuman, since man is made for greater things than the gratification through imperfect and temporal means of his imperfect and temporal senses, which leaves unsatisfied his hunger for total perfection.

What is right with sensuality is that it may be used as a means of contact with the outside world, not as a mere opportunity for egotistic enjoyment, but as a method of understanding how and what to give.

Sensuality is not the same as sensitivity, for the latter is purely passive, mere potential receptivity which exists as well in a radio or a measuring instrument as in man. Sensuality adds to sensitivity the human touch of vital contact, of involvement with world and neighbor. It is through sensuality properly used that we learn to be grateful for God's natural gifts, and most of all for the gift of sex. If we are moved and excited and exalted at the thought of successful sexual meetings, this is no cause for shame: sensuality here is legitimate and good, being a natural condition of the full union of man and wife. The more we feel and sense and enjoy the act of love, the closer we come to each other and the more reason we have for praise and gratitude.

Sensual pleasure in the game of love was planned by God, not for the gratification of sinners, but for the holy fun of the children of light. It is by usurpation that sinners call it their own, and by complete misunderstanding that "spiritual" counselors disparage it. The right thing to do is to return to sanity and true sanctity by receiving gracefully and giving generously all that is good in God's gift. This means, perhaps, changing our whole attitude toward sex, shedding layer after layer of negative, narrowing prejudice by which we have been taught to see in it something not quite right, some lurking danger to mind and soul. There is, in fact, much greater danger to mind and soul in sensual starvation than in sensual development, for, while it is possible to refuse nature what it needs, this same nature takes its revenge by embittering life.

Lust may be a capital sin, but lustiness is a natural virtue — and no supernatural virtue can rest on a denial of the natural. Instead of rejecting the gifts of nature as Satan's work, it is much wiser, more human and more effective to find out how much of them may be accepted as a perfect gift from the Father of Lights, worthy of our attention and of the baptism of Christ.

In many instances, the gap between hedonist and ascetic consists in nothing but a chasm of mutual distrust made up of each party's exaggerated contempt for the excesses and in-adequacies of the other. It is subhuman to confine man's life to the immediately and materially useful and enjoyable, but it is also subhuman to imprison it in a false ideal of disincarnate and artificial perfection. The road to harmony and peace, the Tao, consists in a true and complete balance of all that is human.

One of the happy trends of our time is precisely to reconsider whatever is good in the natural and pagan worlds, thus escaping from the ghetto of unrealism that has been falsely presented as the Christian way of life. As there is a Christian Yoga, there is also a Christian eroticism — which will scandalize only those who need to be shaken out of their spiritual complacency and natural ignorance: those who scorn sexual love, thus naïvely disclaiming their own birthright. Said the caterpillar, seeing a butterfly for the first time, "You'll never get *me* to fly in *that* thing!"

The true philosophy of existentialism, as seen for instance in its Eastern form in Zen Buddhism, comes to the help of those who seek perfection in and through marriage. It is only by means of self-awareness and self-realization — combined with self-renunciation — that we may begin to be ourselves, to com-municate with the world, with our neighbors, and, most of all, with the closest, most constant neighbor, the sexual partner. It is here that the reality of *being* should take precedence over the illusion of *having*, here that the mad trend toward material possessions should be replaced by a peaceful enjoyment of what we are.

The natural goodness of sex, as part of total love, appears also in the fact that sex satisfies man's desire for perpetuation and multiplication of self in the partner and in the offspring. Since qualitative perfection is impossible in the creature, an outlet is offered to reason's natural tendency toward the infinite in the form of quantitative procreation in thought, love and generation. No creature is ever statically complete: every rational creature tends toward progress. This progress, brought about by moral virtue and resulting in sensual and intellectual happiness, consists in the ascent of a dynamic life which multiplies thoughts and actions in the upward direction of personal fulfillment. Pleasure in sex is no fortuitous occurrence: when the act is properly performed, it corresponds very closely with the rational tendency toward perfection of self through multiplication in the other. This multiplication or increase occurs on two levels: on that of the partners, it completes each one through the other; on that of the offspring, it perpetuates both.

XIV

 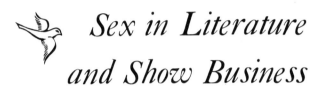

Sex in Literature and Show Business

"Beauty, nakedness, dancing, music, love: can those be among the materials of which holiness is made?"

GERALD VANN, O.P.

There are three main aspects of the literature of sex, the theological, the clinical and the artistic.

True theology considers the complete man and woman in their relationship to God. As we have seen, many theologians have unfortunately followed the doctrine of excessive separation of body and soul: they have exalted the spirit and scorned the flesh.

The clinical approach is the exact reverse, studying the body without respect for the soul. Even psychiatrists are often more concerned with the materialistic pathology of Freud than with an objective appraisal of the body/soul complex.

Artistic literature alone seems able to provide a more-or-less-complete picture of the sexual relationship, for it considers man and woman as whole and living entities.

What, then, of the artistic literature of love? The field open to creative imagination is boundless, for it is graced with the deepest, most lyrical and affective human experiences, with

emotion and crisis, hope and despair, fulfillment and disappointment, all of which make up the tragedies and comedies of life
and are as manifold and enigmatic as the person. Every love
life is creation rediscovered and played anew for better or for
worse, but always intensely, passionately, even in utter failure.
For it moves man and woman to the core and plays upon
vital energies.

There is a great depth of tragedy even in the gray lives of
those who have never truly loved, for the greater the contrast
between what a man seeks and what he finds, the more poignant
the drama. This accounts for the wealth of literary subjects
provided by the drab and dreary mass of those who have been
cheated or have cheated themselves of the glories of life.

How much do we find in all this that may serve as a guide to
our own life? In many instances there arises little more than an
unbearable stench of uncleanliness, sin and despair, particularly
in much of what is being written now. Some vitally moving
and magnificent books have described all too well many a
form of human weakness, but why have so few touched upon
love as it should be played before the eyes of God? Are the
children of light so timid as to be afraid of their sexuality — or
have they been told that God blushes every time they speak of
the pleasure of their matings?

Why the constant prejudice that fun is found in sin alone?
To be sure, the sexual relationship is personal, intimate and
sacred. But is that any reason to let the depraved scoop its
splendor and mix it with their filth? Why has erotica become
synonymous with pornography, if not because too few will
admit that the flowering of physical love is positively virtuous?
Both Eros and Aphrodite are here to stay. Of the whole pagan
pantheon, the symbols of pleasurable love and of feminine
beauty are the only ones to have had their share in the Good
News, for they were invited to Cana and sanctified by a sacrament which recognizes in them a sign of valid and healthy
humanity.

The choice is not between a vital and exciting life of sin and a dull and deadly practice of virtue: all the deadliness and dullness are a direct effect of sin, for, when sex is abused, it is also reduced to a point where it cannot possibly satisfy man's natural and supernatural craving for all-perfect bliss. Instead of being a royal road to mutual perfection, it becomes a dead end of mutual destruction.

If the way of virtue often seems so dreary, it is because of the teaching of pessimists who believe that virtue cannot be pleasurable, nor pleasure virtuous. Pleasure, precisely, is the fruit of virtue: it is the natural result of doing well and easily what needs to be done; it is the reward of an acquired habit patiently formed through learning and experience; it is the elusive flash of recognition of God's glory in the proper doing of what we are called upon to do.

Why should the poetry of sex be almost exclusively the playground of libertines? They are too often the only ones to sing of it openly. Again, why? The deep and more intimate aspects of love are so powerfully lyrical as to be worthy of the attention of the best poets — who should be relieved of any trace of puritanical taboo.

The poets and artists of true love have much more to say than the counterfeiters and the vendors of vice. Every young soul is born with a yearning for love, clean and beautiful. If such yearning is not satisfied with expressions of excellent art — I mean art that is lively, vital, vibrant with the glory that is life — many will fall under the spell of sinful pleasure. For no man can live without love, and it is because of the tragic lack of the right kind of literature that so many of our generation, in their search for the meat of life, fall prey to the exploiters of vice.

Who is more to blame, the publishers of sex trash or the holy weakling so terrified by the powers of his body that he remains as mute and uncreative as a fish? The producer of the sex trash, at least, is doing something: he is answering a need, although he is doing it in the wrong way. It is for us, then, to realize the actuality of this need and to offer artistic fare good enough to put the vice king out of business. But first we must take one great leap out of our fishbowl and learn to breathe!

Literature, and more precisely poetry, may serve as a perfectly legitimate channel for the expression of the joys and emotions of sex. Listen to E. E. Cummings:

> i like my body when it is with your
> body.   It is so quite a new thing.
> Muscles better and nerves more.
> i like your body.   i like what it does,
> i like its hows.   i like to feel the spine
> of your body and its bones, and the trembling
> -firm-smoothness and which i will
> again and again and again
> kiss,   i like kissing this and that of you,
> i like, slowly stroking the, shocking fuzz
> of your electric fur, and what-is-it comes
> over parting flesh. . . . And eyes big love-crumbs,
>
> and possibly i like the thrill
>
> of under me you so quite new.[1]

If such a delicate and charming expression of love gives rise to anything but a feeling that this indeed is joyful and good, if such a gem produces in the mind the slightest reaction of disgust, it is a sure sign of the presence of some persistent negative prejudice that needs to be expelled.

There is here not the slightest indecency and not a trace of obscenity. Obscenity is the same as dirt: it is dirt in terms of sex. Now, dirt is very much a matter of circumstances. Take the purest milk and pour it on a rug: you have dirt. Take some

---

[1] Copyright, 1925, by E. E. Cummings. Reprinted from his volume *Poems, 1923-1954*, by permission of Harcourt, Brace & World, Inc.

of the purest and richest soil, nature's great source of living matter, mix with a little pure rainwater and smear on your shoes: you have dirt again. Now, take sex, a pure gift of God, and seek to satisfy it out of order, when and where it does not belong: you have dirt, obscenity. But to call obscene what are actually effective and delicate representations of love offered in the context of a book of poems is to imply intrinsic dirt in the love relationship itself.

May the reader who does not need this little sermon forgive me. As for the one who does need it, may he forgive himself for any past misunderstanding.

Let us always remember that we are indeed in a fallen state; that our will has been weakened and made prone to abuse; that we cannot rashly gather and enjoy all the fruits of the earth and all the creations of the mind. But let us approach any accessible splendor of this kind with a holy and grateful will, knowing full well that it is but a sign and a foretaste of that pleasure which is God: for then we are free to take to ourselves the beautiful works of nature and man and to treasure them in our hearts.

Unfortunately, from the mass of "frank" literature, there arises, all too often, not the glorious and happy freedom of unfettered life, but the stench of a subhuman state. The protagonists of popular best sellers are all too often a pair of very dull fornicators on whose petty affair great talent is wasted.

In much of the literature of our time, sex is approached with a brutal realism that reduces it to the level of the physiological. Since this is all too limited for men, who because of their very nature cannot extinguish their need for the absolute, there is much demand for an added "kick," for a negative absolute, and this leads to the production of works describing love in its pathological aspects. Once the first step downward has been taken, it is hard to stop the descending spiral which ends in the pit of satanic abuse.

There are also many examples of an entirely different literature of love, lighthearted and amusing, which attracts by its liveliness and youthful spirit, its natural candor and Riviera flavor, its mixture of cocktails and bikinis, of Vespas and virgins, in a merry whirl of sexual enchantment. In a fairyland of vacation resorts, innocent or sophisticated youths and maidens romp under the sun in an atmosphere of uninhibited and Eden-like happiness. This is "the Life," the freedom of total enjoyment which appeals to the many held down by the fetters of reality.

Such fairy tales show love as a happy and irresponsible relationship open to all but narrow-minded fools, a gamboling of suntanned bodies, a play of emotions with no relation whatsoever to moral law. The South Sea myth is exploited in full, as if it were the answer to every man's hunger for perfect love and to every man's dissatisfaction with the state of this fallen world. Because no reference is ever made to broken lives, unwed mothers, abortion, or other unpleasant aspects of brainless love, the reader is left with the depressing feeling that he or she has lost all the fun of life.

Such literature may be even more damaging than the realistic description of sexual evil, for its levity distorts the truth by making of love a farce, spiced with modern wit, in which erotic partners gather the fruits of Eden at no cost. It presents true love as old-fashioned and outdated and plays havoc with emotions by suggesting that freedom is a far better way of life.

The same two approaches, the "heavy" and the "light," are found in show business, both on stage and screen. The motive is generally commercial, sex being used mostly for the sake of attracting customers and making money out of the exploitation of their natural instincts.

From the viewpoint of our study, there is one particular aspect that is specially revealing. By a strange aberration, what is called "wicked" in sexy shows does not correspond at all with true sexual disorder or sin. A clear example may be found in a slogan which often recurs in some form or other: "God created woman, but the Devil made X." Now, how does the wicked

show featuring Miss X differ from others that are not so qualified? Merely in that natural love play is brashly and provoca-
tively shown in scenes in which there is not the slightest evil —
excepting the fact that, in true show-business tradition, the
lovers are generally illegitimate. An open mind may consider
such scenes as genuinely beautiful expressions of passion. What
is called wicked and attributed to the Devil consists in erotic
pranks that would have been perfectly innocent in the intimacy
of married life. And they are called wicked, not because they
may be damaging to some immature viewer, but precisely because they are delightful!

The sexy shows whose main attraction is their claim to
wickedness may be filled with actual examples of sin — adultery,
lust, sexual abuse, moral corruption — but the attribute of
wickedness is not applied to this veritable evil since other films
that display the same vices are not called wicked or sinful.
Wickedness, then, in the mind of the moronic promoter and
viewer, consists very simply in erotic love play! Love and
pleasure must be accompanied with guilt!

Such is a form of automatic punishment imposed upon impure minds. Because they have lost the true notion of sin and
evil, they see the devil in natural pleasures; because they have
killed in themselves the distinction between right and wrong,
they irrationally deprive themselves of an actual good.

If there are wickedness and sin in the shows that feature sex
too openly, it is not in the naturalistic performance of the
actors, but in the toleration or even glorification of what is
truly opposed to the moral law; and in the irresponsible greed
of producers and distributors who offer such advanced fare to
young people who can readily turn it into occasions of sin.

Writers and producers who take advantage of human weakness and sexual hunger and make of it the habitual subject of
their work show dubious taste. If they are exploiting concupiscence systematically, they belong to the ranks of corruptors and
givers of scandal of whom Christ spoke in just and dreadful
anger. Much of the blame, however, falls on the spectators

who, by their constant patronage, support the multiplication of works of bad morals and bad taste.

One of the direct consequences of the fall — and one of the most easily spotted effects of concupiscence — is the attraction of the forbidden fruit. The tremendous psychological appeal of the sinful, the unclean, the hidden and the shameful is the very antithesis of the tendency toward our proper end. In its lighter aspect, it is expressed in the popular and wistful saying: "Everything I like is either illegal, immoral or fattening!" In its deeper sense, it is a sort of morality in reverse, a cult of disorder, a pursuit of the subhuman. In its extreme form, it is truly satanic, for the Devil makes powerful use of any weakness brought about by man's original failure — to the point of changing the thirst for God and for his Spirit into a thirst for anything that opposes God and denies his Spirit.

The fact of this appeal is all too clear and too well known to commercial exploiters, who cultivate with great talent the art of making money out of displays of immorality, presented either as the liberation from obsolete rules or precisely as the forbidden fruit so eagerly sought by the crowd.

It is these abuses as they exist in the motion-picture industry that are being fought by means of censure and censorship. Movements such as the Legion of Decency, which attempt to overcome this immorality, may be excellent in their intentions, but are poor substitutes for the right kind of education. A well-formed conscience develops aversion for anything truly sinful and indecent. If young people were brought up with a better sense of respect for life and love, there would be little need for prohibitions and moral ratings. Since they are not, such prohibitions and moral ratings may procure some measure of good, at least in the more submissive and obedient.

Yet, an unfortunate result of any kind of classification is to produce the exact opposite of the censor's expectation: for it does little more than focus attention upon the condemned films. Many young viewers seem to consult the ratings for no other reason than to select the shows of the lowest possible grade in the hope of obtaining from them the greatest "kick." In the absence of ratings, they would have been exposed to the average; but, *because of the ratings*, they are able unerringly to choose the worst!

XV

Sex in Representative Art

"All beauty in animals and plants alike is a lasting
and naked form of love and desire."

RAINER MARIA RILKE

There is an immense gap between true art and the prevailing
religious style — the nineteenth-century pietistic realism as seen
on Barclay Street in New York, around St. Sulpice in Paris, and
in every other religious center in the Western world. Popular
Catholic art — with some few exceptions attributable generally
to the Order of St. Benedict — corresponds to a form of expression whose only valid claim to catholicity is the universality of
bad taste. It is a sad thing, for instance, that in the home of a
Catholic family in Japan the only object of glaring ugliness happens to be a picture of the Sacred Heart.

Any truly great art is catholic; that is, universal. Any truly
great art is also religious in that it is true to the image of God
in man. There is no separation between pure art and religious
art, as there is no opposition between true science and religion,
for art is pure and science is true only in so far as they represent
the One, the True, and the Good — that is, the three metaphysical attributes of being. Science and religion have but one
object, reality, but they consider it from different viewpoints.
Science sees reality in its created effects and religion in its absolute Self. Pure art and religious art also have but one object:

beauty — that is, the representation of reality under its aesthetic aspects. On the secondary level, that of use, pure art and religious art may differ, for what is fitting in a bedroom or a museum may not be fitting in a church. The same distinction applies to any form of art, pictorial, plastic, literary, musical, and all others, because there are two values in any artistic expression: the objective, or intrinsic, and the subjective, or affective, the latter being the effect produced on the onlooker or audience. A work of art of great beauty may be dangerous for the young or the simpleminded. This, however, is no reason to condemn it absolutely: it should be used in accordance with its potential good instead of rejected because of its potential evil.

The connecting point between sex and art is usually the naked body, along with any representation of physical love, from the kiss to copulation. The key to proper judgment in the matter seems to be the same as that of shame.

Shame entered the world with original sin. It consisted particularly in the urge to cover the body, and more specifically, the sexual organs. "Then the eyes of both were opened, and they knew that they were naked; and they sewed fig leaves together and made themselves aprons. . . . And the Lord God made for Adam and for his wife garments of skins, and clothed them" (Gen. 3:7, 21).

As indicated in the chapter on the Sins of Sex, original sin was certainly not sexual in essence, yet it considerably disturbed the control of sex by the will and opened the door to every abuse. No longer were Adam and Eve in the state of innocence: they passed from the guilelessness of nudity to the *potential* sinfulness of the naked state. The need for clothing perceived by Adam and Eve extends to all their offspring, liable with them to the same penalties of concupiscence, suffering and death.

A recent development in exegesis sheds an interesting light on the sexual overtone of the story of the fall. Some authors believe that this particular emphasis may be the result of an

178 THE FLOWERING OF SEX

attempt by the sacred writer to fight the sexual disorders of his own time. The text of Genesis is of very recent date when compared to the origin of human life: it is enormously more distant from the birth of mankind than it is from us — most probably by millions of years. There would be no reason for wonder, even in the case of an inspired writer, if his work reflected both the immensely ancient origin of the species and the circumstances of his own time. This, then, may explain in part the insistence of Genesis on the notion of shame, and it may also serve as one more argument against the thesis that original sin vitiated sex in its essence.

It is worth repeating here that original sin affected the will, and not the senses as such. Hence, it is in relation to the will that we must consider sex and nudity, both in themselves and in their artistic representation.

Besides its erotic quality, the human body has an artistic value which makes of it a masterpiece in its own right, a creation of great harmony, an object of aesthetic delight. Any representation of it through an artistic medium is good as long as the intention of the artist is one of admiration, gratitude or elevation — and not a provocation to lust or the distortion of the temple of the Holy Spirit into a diabolical form. The fact that for some narrow minds a statue of naked beauty or a painting of great sensuous merit may become an occasion of impure thoughts or deeds should not weigh on the artist's conscience: for the good of producing a thing of beauty, of expressing a valid creative power, outstrips by far the potential scandal to some poor soul obsessed by sexual sin. There is no justification, for instance, for the prude whose hobby consists in trousering the classics.

The human body, clothed or unclothed, is holy and clean as such. But so much filth has been heaped upon it that nothing but a truly pure heart will restore the original marvel. One of the tasks of both artist and writer is to make of sexed nudity a genuine servant of man's beatitude.

And so, although the author of a nude work of art may be

blameless in the act of artistic creation, he must be prudent in the display of it, the greatest prudence and restraint applying to any representation of sexual love.

In April of 1964, Ron Boise, a young sculptor from Colorado, exhibited eleven metal sculptures in a San Francisco gallery. He was promptly arrested and his sculptures were seized. His work is astonishingly beautiful. It very frankly represents a couple in a variety of sexual attitudes inspired by the *Kama Sutra*. How this can be done movingly, convincingly and aesthetically by no other means than welded fragments of junked cars will remain the artist's secret: but there is no doubt that he has achieved something good. The main danger is that images have a strong motive power: we tend to enact what we see, and the representation of such emotionally packed attitudes is immensely suggestive. But that, precisely, is also their virtue: in their right context, these sculptures may be understood as a paean to sex, as a proposition to do well what needs to be done, as an incentive to the consummation of holy desire. They are love offerings, to be seen and received as such. But their public display will be possible only in a world less ashamed of itself. If sexual love is good, its image also will be good if offered with reverence and truth. These conditions have been fully met, for instance, in Eric Gill's illustrations for the *Song of Songs*.[1]

The same principles apply to literature. The author of a lively and beautiful account of love play has produced a work of positive moral virtue, for the thing described is good and its description is a legitimate means of artistic expresson. If offered in the right circumstances, the description even of sinful acts may be good, for there is no obligation on the part of the writer to confine his efforts to hagiography.

From the viewpoint of the reader, the morality of a book depends upon his intention when he reads it and upon the moral effect he may foresee. A realistic description of the most praiseworthy love presented with literary skill and good taste may

[1] Waltham St. Lawrence, Berkshire: The Golden Cockerell Press, 1935.

throw an unprepared youth into a state of dangerous emotional disturbance and be a direct occasion of disorder. This, again, should not weigh on the writer's conscience, for he is not responsible for the lack of education or understanding of his readers. Some of the responsibility here lies with the distributors, but mostly with the authorities — parental, religious, or educational — who should see to it that young minds are offered the proper fare.

An interesting study remains to be made of the relationship between beauty and sexual attraction, since it is a very important aspect of the problem of love. It has its roots in the deepest recesses of nature, in the very laws by which living beings tend naturally to the perfection of their species.

Were it not for adverse external circumstances, every tree and every plant would be a perfectly healthy, balanced and fruitful specimen of its species. But the seed may be weakened from having been produced by imperfect parents; excessive or insufficient warmth or moisture may have hampered its normal development; soil conditions, poverty of nutrients, lack of some minerals, sandy or gravely texture may have imposed further restrictions on growth; lack of air, space and light due to narrow or shady location and competition with other plants may have further decreased a seedling's chances of developing into a perfect adult. Adding to that the damage done by microorganisms, insects, birds and other animals, including man, it is a wonder that any tree ever grows to be the deserving object of Joyce Kilmer's praise.

The reason why, in spite of every obstacle, a tree often does grow to be a thing of beauty is the stubborn, innate tendency toward perfection which is the principle that makes the seed rise from its dark and humid tomb, the seedling reach up toward the sun, and the tree itself grow for the glory of God and the service and happiness of man.

Each man and woman, likewise, is the summary of every preceding generation with its sufferings and imperfections; and their love is, in spiritual form, that very same principle of perfection which is the primer of all organic growth. Each man and woman unknowingly and instinctively seeks the perfect mate in order to bring forth a perfect race of men. But since mankind is very different from any other living species, the standard of human perfection is influenced by two elements that are not found anywhere else: freedom of choice, which entails error and imperfection, and spiritual values, which may be properly placed above physical characteristics.

Human beauty in its affective aspect — as a determinant of love — is almost completely subjective. Was there ever a body that was not beautiful at least in one aspect to one person? Did any woman ever give birth to a child that was not the most gorgeous infant ever born? The same blindness is found in sexual love. In both instances it is a veil that covers human imperfection for the very practical purpose of ensuring the continuance of the human race, and it is justified because physical perfection is not man's supreme good.

As soon as the mysterious spark of love has been struck, physical beauty becomes of minor importance or even of no importance whatsoever. In some minds it may never have existed at all. This gives as good a chance at marriage to the physically underprivileged as to the modern counterparts of Venus and Adonis.

There is, however, in all higher forms of love a strong desire for perfection in every order, including that of physical conformation. While the true level of beauty is not dependent upon the body alone, which is but a frame, a container, young love that blossoms forth in gloriously handsome bodies has a satisfying and exalting quality that is visible to all. The whole world smiles at lovers, but the whole world rejoices and applauds at the sight of lovers gifted with true beauty. It is in this sense, of rejoicing and applauding, that we may look upon the splendor of human bodies in their artistic representations.

The sexual appeal between a man and a woman depends upon a certain physical harmony which is an expression of the soul. There is here a mysterious concordance perceived in the senses and yet far above the physical level: it rises through the emotional to the intellectual and the spiritual levels. It may result in such uplifting that the sensitive may be led to sing and pray because of the overflowing of their joy, not only in the intimacy of marriage but also at the discovery of some fleeting vision of sexual beauty in some living person or some form of art. It is this enrichment, this intellectualization of the primitive instinct that justifies the nude.

Some of the girls Sam Haskins,[2] the South African photographer, captured with his magic camera are unforgettable signs of wholesome and pure delight, of the wonder of being woman, and beautiful, and of rejoicing in young life. There is no reason to overlook the fact that they may be marvelous partners in the game of love, for it is quite obvious and obviously part of their beauty. What must be done, however, is to eliminate any appropriating greed. If this is asking too much, if every sensuous form is inevitably an occasion of sin, let us be brutally iconoclastic. But if the vision of sacred and vital beauty and liveliness in their natural context may be an occasion of exalting and grateful happiness, then it is but obscurantism to seek the destruction or hiding of such a marvel.

Many have been poisoned with untruth to the point of being unable to take in their stride, and enjoy with a pure mind and a clean heart, the aesthetically satisfying expressions of sensuous beauty. They seem to believe that by making man sensitive to it God made a major mistake, which he is always trying to correct by imposing rigorous asceticism on every candidate to perfection. St. Bernard did well by his own lights when he closed his eyes so as not to enjoy the beauty of the lakes of Switzerland, for there is immense redemptive value in the heroic renunciation of such men of prayer: but extreme asceticism cannot serve as a foundation to every man's sanctity.

[2] *Five Girls* (New York: Crown Publishers, 1962), and *Cowboy Kate* (New York: Crown Publishers, 1965).

Asceticism is a means, not an end. What is praiseworthy is holy renunciation of something known to be good, a renunciation which derives, not from a perverse refusal of God's gifts, but from the search for some higher good. False and puritanical asceticism consists in running away from an actual good, and the precise point where the error is compounded is the belief that pleasure itself is wicked. There is an utterly false and inhuman perfection in the flight from pleasure in general, sex in particular, and from the artistic expression of both.

The puritanical mind is iconoclastic and grim. It lives in a dull and cruel world devoid of any emotion but fear; it is a prisoner of its own prejudice, forever offended by what should be sheer delight, and scandalized at the sight of the children of freedom wholeheartedly enjoying everything good. The puritanical mind cannot reach the understanding that the Trinity is the source and supreme end of all delight, and that, while the sexual mystery is sacred, not every one of its expressions must necessarily be covered with a veil.

There is a good — and mysterious — power in woman that takes man's breath away or induces him to write lyric poetry or again leads him to the highest exaltation. It is not femininity as such, but particular signs of harmony, imaginary or real, a secret communication established with some expressive image, enhanced a thousand times by the difference of sex. It may be nothing more than the tracing of a few lines projecting that by which woman is desirable and good. Some may react in a gross and material way, but the sensitive may perceive in artistic beauty a spark of the divine light itself, a glimpse of unearthly perfection in and through the most earthly form. And the marvel is that the more of earthly, sensuous perfection seen in the form, the greater the exaltation in the mind.

True elevation of the sexual instinct consists in making of the instinctual attraction something much more than a preparatory phase of copulation. Because sex is one of the major motive powers of the body/spirit complex, its emotions are perceived in both spheres. Nothing we do and nothing we think is ever done or thought in the spirit or in the flesh alone. At the sight of artistically and sexually appealing beauty which rings in us a sudden clamor of bells, we, being civilized, do not react solely in terms of physical desire: our whole being is lifted up by the vision of something both sacred and good.

And so, since all activities leading to the legitimate and full consummation of love are themselves legitimate and even virtuous, contemplation of the aesthetic qualities of the nude is naturally good — although it may become an *occasion* of evil when the will is not properly disposed.

The use of the semi-naked female body as a promotion gimmick for the sale of anything from a deodorizer to a deluxe automobile is now so much taken for granted that it has ceased to astonish. This, again, is a commercial exploitation of the sexual instinct.

It may seem strange at first to realize that in our modern world so much emphasis has been placed on the female body and so little on the male. This is the exact opposite of what happens in the case of primitive man and in the animal world, where the male has the brilliant feathers and all the trimmings. In our time, it is the female who displays a fireworks of color and appears in the gaudiest *déshabillé* in real life and in every form of art. There seem to be many reasons for this. The first and most obvious is that the world as we know it, the world of real life and of art, is a world dominated by men, whose interest is centered upon the opposite sex. Although perceptive of the aesthetic qualities of the male body, these men refrain from emphasizing it through a conscious or unconscious effort to avoid any reproach about homosexuality. Again, although female sensuality may be inflamed as intensely as that of the male, there is great reluctance on the part of women to admit it blatantly, so that female artists seldom offer renderings of the male figure. All this makes for a world dominated, from the billboard to the museum, by the female body.

Dualism of Humanity

"Sexual dualism is an invitation to the dialogue of love."   PAUL ANCIAUX

In every culture and religion of the world, sexual dualism is acknowledged as one of the major human factors, one of the deep mysteries of life very closely related to the sacred. In the ancient traditions of China and Mesopotamia, in Egypt with Ra and Isis, in India with Siva and Devi, the different aspects of the male and female principles gave rise to countless instances of sexual symbolism and innumerable sexed deities. In almost every early culture, there seem to have been a male sky god and a female earth goddess. Much of this has been intensively studied, but so great is the number of manifestations of reverence and wonder before sex and so rich their artistic expression that much research of great interest remains to be done.

Limiting ourselves at present to the mythologies more closely related to our own culture — the Greek and the Roman — we distinguish immediately a strong sexual differentiation among the higher gods, Zeus and Hera dominating the Greek Pantheon, and their counterparts, Jupiter and Juno, presiding over that of Rome. In both cultures, erotic love is personified and made divine in the ideal female, in the Greek Aphrodite and the Roman Venus — who may be seen as symbols of lust, but also, and in a much more kindly and satisfying way, as representations of perfect love in the highest form accessible to the pagan mind: physical beauty.

Parallel to the worship of idealized love, the worship of sex as such assumed a more direct and materialistic form in the phallic and Priapean rites in the two classical cultures. The ancients were concerned with sex not so much in its erotic aspect as in its relationship to life and fecundity. The Greek dionysiac processions, in which these rites were performed, celebrated originally the sacredness of every form of birth. They were held in anticipation of an abundant harvest and of the multiplication of chattel, or in thanksgiving for them. Human fecundity merely received its share in the paeans addressed to bountiful nature. The greater dionysiac processions took place at the end of March, celebrating the emergence of new life; the lesser processions, in December, at the testing of the new wine. The Romans held parallel ceremonies in honor of Cybele, the Great Mother Earth. In both cultures, it was only toward the end that fecundity rituals degenerated into licentiousness and orgies.

Much of what is valid in sexual symbolism may be found in the Christian religion. Ra, the male sun god of the Egyptians, the Greek Helios and the Roman Apollo remind us of the Sun of Justice; the feminine Isis, the Moon, evokes in our mind the Virgin Mary; the Greek and Roman deities of the earth symbolize Holy Mother Church; and their thundering Zeus-Jupiter, in spite of his very human and capricious temper, may be seen as a remote figure of the Father. It is, indeed, because of the representations of Zeus as an imposing and bearded figure that the Father is shown in this way. The comparison must stop here, for never could the gods of love rise above their clay: none of them could be compared even in the remotest manner with the Holy Spirit of Life and Love.

We ourselves are so deeply affected by the dualism of sex that it influences the pattern of our religious thought. We are unable to imagine, or even conceive, a world of spirits without the same distinction as that existing between man and woman. Since the only human way of representing a rational being is to endow it with human form, and every human form is either male or female, we have a tendency to anthropomorphize even bodiless spirits.

The painters of Byzantine icons and several Flemish masters attempted to solve the dilemma by representing sexless figures. Hugo van der Goes, Gerard David and Mabuse, for instance, have given us images of colorful, translucent, floating beings that are neither young men nor young women. But when it comes to the representation of God, the images are consistently male. (The only clear exception seems to be the celebrated Trinity Icon by the Muscovite painter Rublev, which shows the three divine persons as youthful and sexless human forms in the style of Byzantine angels.)

In an early style, now forbidden by the Church, Father, Son and Holy Spirit are shown as three bearded men. The objection to this style seems to have been rather the identical representation of the three distinct persons than the fact that all three were males.

That Christ in his humanity was a male is a fact which permits the artist to represent him as such, but only in so far as he is the Word made flesh. Any representation of the Father as a man, and particularly as an old man, is basically defective, for it excludes from our mind the presence in God's creative power of those perfections which are specifically feminine. Since the complete human being consists in the male-female complex — fulfilled in marriage in an actual way, and in the religious life by proper recognition and sublimation — any representation of God that is exclusively male leaves us with a feeling of uneasiness. Several writers since early times have attempted to attribute feminine characteristics to the Holy Spirit, but this is no improvement, for it produces the same ill effect in reverse and places between two of the divine persons — the male Father and the female Spirit — an imaginary opposition and complementing which implies some lack of perfection

THE FLOWERING OF SEX

in both. That is why there is so much wisdom in the approach of a contemporary Chinese scholar, Doctor John C. H. Wu, who always addresses God as "Our Motherly Father" — without knowing that in this he is following St. Francis de Sales.

Chinese art has given us one of the most striking graphic symbols of sexual dualism, the yin-yang, a circle consisting of interlocking, black and white, symmetrical figures. The Chinese male, with the greater physical strength and proportionate smugness of his sex, considers the "yin," or female principle, to be dark, passive and evil, while the masculine "yang" is light, active and beneficial. The whole symbol, however, indicates that the perfection of humanity, represented by the circle, implies the simultaneous and closely intertwined presence of *both* principles in *both* man and woman.

It seems to be a law of nature that man goes out into the world and battles for his own development and survival and those of his brood, while woman attends to matters more directly related to the inner life of the family. Man spends most of his time among strangers; woman lives in the tight circle of her immediate relatives and neighbors.

While some women challenge men on their own ground, acquiring skills that for centuries had seemed to be the prerogative of the male, this does not mean that the order of nature has been changed. Such women are the exception, and few if any ever seem to find complete fulfillment in careers which deprive them of their specific function of giving life and love. They may even be condemning themselves to complete loneliness in their later years.

The natural order, then, outside of the special calling of religious celibacy, still is founded upon the family unit, man, wife and their offspring. Man returns to his home wearing the scars and fatigue of daily battle; woman meets him weighed down by her own load of exhaustion. And it is this wounded man and this tired woman who meet in the conjugal bed. Both have great need of assistance and compassion of a kind that none but the other is able to give: the woman needs reassurance of love and proof that her time is not frittered away uselessly; the man needs appeasement and close intimacy to counteract the insecurity produced by a hostile world.

Let them not unload their burdens upon each other, but let each offer instead what the other seeks, and the burdens will vanish. Let them meet on the level of understanding and sympathy and physical closeness, knowing full well that each is both the healer and the healed, and that there is in the offer to heal much more self-healing power than in any whining for help – and a much better preparation for the total surrender of love. If the time is right, let them take each other with the full intent of giving all that love and sex can give – of reassurance to woman and appeasement to man.

Perhaps tiredness is the most frequent state of those truly engaged in life. At times, both husband and wife are so exhausted that no thought of sex enters their minds. Even then they can procure the refreshments and solace of the presence of each other – of each one as other, male and female, completing their human fullness through mutual recognition beyond the haze of pain. The touch of a hand, an arm around a drooping shoulder may work marvels of communion – provided the recipient of these good-intentioned gestures is not feeding the baby or standing over a hot stove.

Domesticity, enslavement to a house, may also be an enemy of love. Every husband would rather have a sparkling wife in a somewhat bedraggled home than a bedraggled wife in a sparkling home. This, as in everything, is a matter of measure. It is part of the quality of a good wife to give her time to what is important, to meet the demand of the most urgent need, which may sometimes be her own freedom. At times, duties and cares will be so urgent that nothing will remain for lighter moments. But let this not become a routine: there is no particular virtue in doing nothing but chores when other and pleasanter activities are at all possible. No fully virtuous wife puts her own freedom and culture, her own charm and her husband's pleasure at the very bottom of the totem pole, as the things least worthy of her consideration and the last to which her strength will go. If she runs out of freedom to be herself, and to think of love, she will soon run out of a husband.

What is important is the element of surprise. Even in the midst of a period of hard work, any wife can find one afternoon to take care of herself, to thoroughly rest and relax, perhaps even inducing the desire to adorn herself with as many graces as nature and artifice permit. No husband would ever complain if from time to time he found himself a *Maja*, whether *vestida* or *desnuda*, on returning home from work.

The natural differences between man and woman, physiological, emotional and intellectual, in no way deprive woman of the right to a personal and intelligent life. Although an all-absorbing career does not seem ideal for her, there are a thousand and one activities that will keep her alert and alive, and I am not referring to bridge clubs or PTA meetings. Her natural creativity may be expressed in a number of ways within the framework of the home and also outside of it, so that she may have a fully rewarding means of self-expression, a world of her own in which to find relief from the labors of raising a family. The feminist movement, while tending to liberate woman from slavery, had a tendency to impose upon her a slavery of a different kind: by opening up careers to her that had been reserved for men, this movement has subjected her to all the harshness and competitive battles of the world of men. It is not there that she will be happy, but in various forms of intellectual and creative life compatible with the love and care of husband and children, which will lift her out of the *hausfrau* drudgery.

Dualism necessarily implies incompleteness. If we admit a distinction between male and female perfections, the ideal being of each sex will lack the specific perfections of the other. Both man and woman are born incomplete, or else God would not have said, "It is not good for man to live alone."

Assuredly, through the grace of the vow of chastity, man without woman and woman without man may attain full human perfection in the sense that they will fulfill their destiny through sublimation. But to say that any human being that lacks intimate correspondence with the opposite sex attains the fullness of human experience is quite another thing. Objectively speaking, it is in the couple that the human fully comes to bloom, man and woman becoming one in spirit, heart and flesh in the union of love. It is love that is their greatness and the measure of their being, that love which is the gift of each one to the other and of both to God.

Let us now consider the dualism of sex on each of three levels, those of spirit, heart and flesh. Dualism on the level of the spirit is marked by the encounter of two free and independent souls within a common bond and for the sake of a common goal. Knowledge comes from sense experience. Now, since the senses operate through instruments composed of cells, every one of which is part of either a man or a woman, the rational method of man and woman will necessarily reflect this difference. Woman, characteristically, is impelled by intuitive leaps and bounds without any apparent logical link. Man must painfully connect link to link before reaching a conclusion, and sometimes he may be infuriated to discover that his wife beats him to the finish by means which seem to him unfair. On the other hand, there are some fields of thought in which a womanly woman is simply not interested, precisely because no progress is possible in them without sustained and organized logic. The point here is not to argue about which one of the two possesses the best instrument of knowledge, but simply to demonstrate one of the effects of dualism in matters that are far above the simply biological.

On the level of the heart, sexual dualism gives rise to a close and warm companionship. When graced with true love, it leads to those refinements of tenderness that soothe and appease, strengthen and support. There is dualism here because of the complementing of each one with the riches of the other: the man providing fortitude and confidence and the woman, reassurance, closeness, consolation . . . and surprise, that delightful spontaneity which strikes the ponderous male as a bolt of lightning and leaves him panting and begging for more!

As for the level of the flesh, dualism is so obvious as to require no comment but this: love elevates and truly spiritualizes what is by nature good and healthy and sound. God made the difference, as he made everything else, out of love; and we are to be grateful for it and to use it according to his will.

Between the original forms of bisexual reproduction and the present manifestations of sexuality in man, there is evidence of a tremendous progress. In original instinctual matings, there was no thought of tenderness, mutual gift, or the fulfillment of each through the powers of the other. Nothing was known of the refinements of love play or of the many ways in which sensual and psychic pleasure may be derived from the sexual difference. What was at first a blind physiological process has now become an attribute of the person, a power with emotional and spiritual implications. Even within the short framework of historical time, there has been discernible improvement in the consciousness of the sexual relationship — a fact which Teilhard de Chardin probably would have noted if his attention had settled on this point. The sexual rites may now be ruled by the highest spiritual ambition and the loftiest desire of personal fulfillment. While procreation, the original effect, is still brought about when desired, other effects have assumed a major importance. The invitation of sexual dualism to the dialogue of love has been answered in full.

☙ XVII

Love and Personality

"... Do not swear at all,
Or if thou wilt, swear by thy gracious self ..."
WILLIAM SHAKESPEARE

The worth of a person is felt in communication with others, for in solitude, in the absence of interchange, there is no point of reference, and hence no proof of value. Again, it is through interchange that impressions are received, thoughts engendered and actions brought to life; and it is in the performance of harmonious actions that pleasure is born.

The delight of interpersonal relationship consists in a mysterious correspondence between individuals who are free to receive and to give. It is found in friendship: the meeting of minds and hearts within a shared sense of truth, beauty and humor, adding proof upon proof that creation is good, that we are part of it, know it and communicate in the knowledge of it. Such communication enriches our own uniqueness with the fruit of other creative and independent minds, each one offering what no other could. Culture and happiness consist in gathering such singular personal contributions into sheaves of golden wheat and bunches of tangy grapes: into substantial food and drink.

It is only through the other that we find ourselves: through communication, then commitment, that we acquire a positive value within the providential plan. Man and woman alone are limited to the all-too-tight frontiers of themselves. What is needed is the breaking of the bonds of self, the rising out of the cocoon of narcissism into the splendor of true love. This may be realized perfectly either in the dedicated lives of religious celibates or in the special relationship of man and wife.

There is a great amount of truth in the Hegelian philosophy of thesis, antithesis and synthesis: it expresses the human contact, the reaction to it, and the consequent gain in experience and merit. The dynamism of life is made up of a succession of personal challenges: of the action of one person upon another, followed by a response, and leaving a residue of growth. The art of life and the art of love consist in making sure that this residue is positive, that it adds to the value of both parties, that it enriches their persons through new experiences. Precisely in that does sexual love serve as a builder of the personality. Each meeting — in the mind, the emotions or the flesh — may become an enrichment if taken for what it is: *a gift*, imperfect in many ways, and yet, when properly accepted, a step forward to wholeness and holiness.

The mystery of sex is but one particular aspect of the mystery of the person: it is part of the universal challenge every man and woman face as soon as they become free to think and act on their own. Sex is not a closed world, a self-sufficient activity, but one particularly important concern among the others of which human destiny is made. It does not contain its own reward, nor can it be sought for itself, for it is an imperfect good — and no imperfect good taken unlimitedly can procure anything but disgust. That is why the sexual life of the playboy is so often a disaster.

Sex, being part of individual life, partakes of individual differences like everything else in man. There are many varieties in the sexual gifts preexisting as natural endowment, and this differentiation is extended by the possible use or abuse of what nature has provided. Sexual development and happiness, then, are dependent in part on inborn potencies, but to a greater degree on each man and woman's pattern of culture, paralleling development in other fields. Since few people are fully gifted by nature, truly knowing and giving, completely generous and alive, there are few perfect marriages. This should not discourage anybody from trying: on the contrary, with a clear knowledge of perfectibility, considerable improvement in the marital relationship is available to every husband and wife provided they are willing to learn and able to try. No marriage is static: even the best needs to move ahead, for there is always room for improvements and increase in understanding and delight.

In the encounter of marriage, interpersonal relationship reaches its highest point — but sometimes also its lowest, for, as Balzac pointed out, in *Le Curé de Tours,* the partners are constantly challenged with an opportunity to grow either in love or hatred for each other. In order to be successful, married life must be approached in a spirit of offering, of attention to true human values and to the partner's gifts. Many a shy and clumsy attempt to love is smothered before it has a chance to bloom. In true love, every small and tentative gift should be collected with care — *colligite fragmenta* — and stored just as carefully. Only then will husband and wife develop progressively that openness of one person before the other that flowers into happiness and gratitude.

Once sexual love is properly understood to be valuable, appeasing and satisfying, once it has been practiced with charitable fire in the person-to-person encounter of lovers whose every movement is transformed into an act of praise and joy, then the clouds of anguish, the feelings of insecurity and guilt melt away in the warmth of what is by essence the most vital human act. As soon as the gates of successful love have been opened, there will always remain in the depths of the lovers' hearts an ardent hope for further adventures, for deeper excursions in the garden of sex. The pleasure itself, being both immense and insufficient, gives rise to ever-increasing desire.

The quality of personal pleasure found in sexual love exceeds by far the Scholastic notion of the three goods of matrimony, *proles, fides* and *sacramentum,* offspring, faithfulness and indissolubility. With its heavy emphasis on duty, this incomplete listing overlooks the more delightful and dynamic aspects of the relationship. Even admitting that the objective end of marriage is the offspring and that marriage itself implies the good of indissolubility (which is the classical interpretation of the word *sacramentum* in the present context), we cannot accept faithfulness as sufficiently broad a term to cover everything else that is good in marriage — all the less since, in Scholastic theory, faithfulness refers merely to the fulfillment of a duty. The act of love is made to be a matter of law, the execution of an obligation, a compulsory service to be rendered on request. Nothing could be more remote from the joyful, personal and spontaneous intimacy of true love.

For the Scholastics, the goods of matrimony consist merely in those advantages that are forced upon every married couple. Among the greater goods they ignore are those which constitute a true marriage: intimacy, companionship, pleasure, mutual awakening and discovery, participation in cosmic life, and the thousand and one revelations born of the union of two potential infinities into a single whole.

The dilemma is clear: either man is made for woman and woman for man in a relation of mutual personal completion that leads to the summit of spiritual, emotional and physical union, through rational, sentimental and erotic love, for the sake of the offspring and of individual fulfillment; or God is deceiving man by attracting him to the performance of sexual acts while forbidding their natural development. If the act itself is good, then everything conducive to it is also good. Pleasure is favorable to both aspects of marriage, for it strengthens companionship in the sweet complicity of shared delight while also procuring a favorable climate for conception, since a woman thoroughly aroused seems in a better condition to conceive than if she were passive and cold.

Thus since, according to theologians, the primary end of marriage is the bringing forth of children, and the full range of love play assists to the reproductive function, there exists such a thing as virtuous eroticism — which should not by any means be called concupiscence: it is a valid, legitimate and meritorious manifestation of love.

It is impossible to have it as the ancients wanted: to assure procreation while scorning its means. Either erotic exaltation is good as conducive to procreation and union; or it is evil, and then its natural effect cannot be the virtuous end of the sacrament of matrimony. The absurdity of the second alternative proves the truth of the first. The sin of sex without procreation has been heavily overemphasized; the sin of procreation *without* sex is never mentioned, and yet there is something repulsive in copulation performed for the sole purpose of breeding, in the absence of any fire of passion.

Because the rightful union of lovers and the bringing forth of their fruit is possible only within marriage, sexual pleasure in its erotic aspects may be sought from no other than the one and only spouse. This, of course, does not mean that a man may not look upon another woman and rejoice at the sight of her without committing adultery in his heart. For he may see her, not as an object of his mating instinct, but as a member of that sex given to him for his joy in a thousand ways besides copulation. It is a poor man indeed whose senses are so brutally volatile that he has no choice but to sin or abstain from the pleasure of woman — and by that I mean everything but what the brute sees in her.

There is something infinitely superior to mere animal instinct in the breathtaking emotion that moves civilized man at the sight of feminine beauty — or civilized woman at the sight of true manliness. Such is but a proof that the creative power and glory of God shine forth in striking fashion through his greatest and noblest creatures.

Our sexual life extends far beyond its obvious consummation. Since all of us are either male or female throughout — with a very few cases of imperfect characterization — there is in our very constitution, in the form of our thoughts and dreams a constant conversation with the opposite sex. Fidelity does not demand such strict control that sexual conversation be limited to the legitimate spouse: a true friendship enhanced by the difference of sex is perfectly possible. It is also quite possible and innocent to enjoy some of those manifestations of sexual beauty that bring to the heart a sudden surge of joy: some fleeting encounter, the passing glance of a perfect stranger, or anything else that proclaims the glory of what is good in woman — even the proud bearing of their sex as a standard of victory revealed in elegant dress, natural poise or well-balanced gait.

All such things are good if we look upon them and accept them, not as temptations, nor as ends in themselves, nor even as substitutes for love, but as reasons for the further enjoyment of love. When such a sight arouses some erotic desire, even this may be good if it is reported to the sacramental partner and serves as a further incentive for the mutual gift. In such incidents, what receives true homage is the flowering in woman of what was promised to man in paradise. He may be enchanted by it without falling into the excesses of carnal guilt; he may also be reassured and sustained by the knowledge that, if such moving grace is but a reflection of God's creative power, the full vision of him must indeed be supremely good.

The proper use of sex is very much a matter of personal culture: since man is both rational and perfectible, all his actions may be progressively improved and elevated in view of his true and final goal. In marriage, the goal is not sexual gratification as such, but mutual assistance toward the achievement of the final end of personal perfection, as regards the lovers themselves, their offspring, and the whole economy of creation.

At times we are so strongly conscious of our personal unity and unicity that we are hardly able to conceive our part in the general plan of the universe. As with young lovers who reject the thought that any other lovers ever existed, so it is with the phenomena of sex in general: the originality and personality of the union often blurs its cosmicity. And yet the civilized use of sex should take into consideration not only the persons of the lovers, but also all future generations in motion toward the Pleroma, the total fulfillment of mankind in the state of glory. Awareness of our participation in this progress may be lost in the thrill and pleasure of sexual adventures. Yet, we should think of this participation in our more sober moments and make of such thought an additional motive for enjoying the game of love to its very heights and depths.

In the close intimacy of wedded life there are large areas of happiness unsuspected by many who live too narrowly. These areas are found in the spiritual union of minds and souls loving personally and distinctly the same absolute, and rejoicing in their common goal; in the union of two sensitive individuals enjoying personally and distinctly the same sense of beauty, while receiving together the constant shower of God's natural gifts; in the total dedication to each other of every sensual power of their most intimate and personal function: sexual love.

Once the relative merit of created and uncreated good has been clearly perceived and the sense of values has been so developed as to make the will conform with reason, every earthly pleasure may be plucked as a delicious fruit, and none more delightfully than sex. Precisely in this is concupiscence overcome by the grace of marriage: desire is not extinguished, but ordained to what is good. And what is good in the act of love is the total impact of its vital glory when it is sought, not as an absolute, but as a gift of God's kindness, a gift we receive both from the Creator and from our chosen mate, a gift we must learn to give and take, a gift we must return to God by using it generously and joyfully. And yet, in the reality of daily life, perfect meetings of man and wife may be so widely spaced as to leave oceans of hunger and sorrow in between.

This may be due, not only to the hardships of life, but also to differences in temperament, in vital rhythm, in the relative importance and urgency that sex assumes in different personalities, and at different times within the same person. Seldom do husband and wife have an exactly balanced desire, and even if they do, both will follow a fluctuating pattern of eagerness and indifference that seldom coincides.

Even then, there is still place for joy, for the greatest joy is not the gratification of our own instincts, but the perception — rational, emotional and physical — of the peace and happiness we are able to procure and of which we sense the flowering in the personal object of our love. As always, true love is altruistic: there is more joy in giving than in receiving. But there is supreme joy in a mutual gift. And there is much giving, not only in the rare moments of total fulfillment, but also in the fact of mutual forbearance and respect, in careful consideration for each other's successive waves of tiredness or desire.

Why fritter life away in useless longing for an impossible perfection? Why relegate happiness to some nonexistent future? Instead of pining after what we hope will come next week or next year, let us enjoy whatever the present contains: it is all we will ever have. If a full sexual festival is not on the program of the moment, let us think of the incredible privilege of the willing and loving company of a woman, of being together in love, even without a sign, a word or a touch, just knowing together that the whole thing was wonderful, is wonderful, and will continue to be wonderful as long as each is present to the other, each willing and eager to comply with the other's needs; and that with a little patience all the stars of heaven will again come tumbling down, often at a moment when we least expect it.

The only reasonable attitude toward lovemaking is a grateful acceptance of whatever comes our way, and not an expectation of paradise. Let us then take nothing for granted, consider nothing as our absolute right; let us accept wholeheartedly the moments of happiness, and learn to take without pained surprise the days and months and perhaps even years of sorrow; let us demand nothing of our partner or of providence, and yet be ever ready to receive everything. Then only shall we be without bitterness, and truly grateful for the surprise of joy.

 XVIII

Perfecting the Act of Love

"What we really need are a few sexy saints."
ANNE MARTIN

In his speech to Italian midwives, Pope Pius XII advises:

> Banish from your minds the cult of pleasure and do your best to stop the diffusion of literature that thinks it a duty to describe in full detail the intimacy of conjugal life under the pretext of instructing, directing and reassuring. To calm the timid consciences of couples, common sense, natural instinct, and a brief instruction on the clear and simple maxims of Christian morality are usually sufficient.

The Pope is condemning those works whose main purpose is the promotion of irresponsible hedonism and proposing the means "to calm the timid consciences of couples." But are such means sufficient preparation for marriage? What of those couples whose conscience has been duly calmed? Is a peaceful conscience enough to make a success out of marriage? Could the newlywed know from instinct how to behave when instinct, debased by theologians who call it concupiscence, is further vitiated by an overwhelming mass of distortions and bad examples? What "brief instruction on the clear and simple maxims of Christian morality" would ever suffice to launch young

people safely on the matrimonial road? And are the principles
of Christian morality really clear and simple? As presently expressed they are overly clear and overly simple, lacking in both
realism and charity. To rely on them and on distorted sexual
instincts amounts to depriving young lovers for long or forever
of the full flowering of their God-given relationship, and imposing upon them instead the burden of the primitive — as if
the whole sexual pattern of civilized man had not benefited by
a progressive "hominization," to borrow one of Teilhard de
Chardin's favorite expressions. Such progress has not become
part of instinct, but must be learned, as must everything else
that makes man superior to animal.

When the violence of instinct, seeking complete satisfaction,
is faced with inadequate instruction, the result is either unbridled lust, when such instruction is bypassed, or crippling
inhibition, when it is retained. Every young married couple has
a human right to full knowledge and enlightenment in the art
of love. Inadequate instruction may lead to irreparable blun-
ders, to exaggerated demands amounting at times to first-night
rape, followed by complete frustration and frigidity. At the
very least, lack of information allows potentially excellent lovers
to flounder in clumsy experiments instead of progressing together with the help provided by centuries of human experience.

Some few gifted couples with an uncommon sense of measure, creative imagination and vigorous unspoiled natural powers
may eventually attain, without help, a happy sexual relationship. But in our world, in which sex is warped both by hedonistic exaggeration and puritanical shame, and the natural has
given way to the unnatural and artificial, there is an absolute
need for a much more complete education than a simple and
brief instruction in matters of right and wrong.

Erotic love is a human and rational activity open to unlimited
perfectibility. It must be learned and improved, and this cannot be done without external help. There is need, then, not for
the *Kama Sutra* or any other manual of systematic and for-

malized pleasure-seeking, but for a treatise on what is truly refined and civilized in the whole relationship.

Every instinct needs to be developed. Any seemingly automatic function that is not purely vegetative must be enlightened by reason and directed by free will. Chewing and eating, for instance, are instinctive processes. Yet, in the choice, preparation and use of food there is a broad field of gastronomic art and acquired knowledge. In terms of sex, the same need of rationalizing instinct is present in an even more obvious way: what is instinctual and animal must be made personal and human.

In the common treasury of mankind, there is a wealth of recordings related to the proper use of the sexual function. It is contained in the literature of love. As we have seen, this literature is enormous and so much under the influence of pagans, hedonists and libertines as to resemble more closely an ill-smelling swamp than a safe and rational road to personal happiness. Materialistic treatises abound in precise details on the physiology and psychology of sex, but almost exclusively with a single end in view: the procuring of maximum pleasure at minimum cost in terms of responsibility and personal engagement. They lead to the false notion that constant and perfect bliss is obtainable at will through the development of physiological skill, with any partner at all, in marriage or in occasional affairs. Seldom do these works reach the recognition of emotional needs, hardly ever do they rise to the level of an encounter of persons, and they never consider sex in terms of spiritual values or in relation to man's eternal destiny.

The most frequent error consists in overlooking the fact of original sin by assuming that an earthly paradise is within easy grasp of anyone unscrupulous and skillful enough to pluck its random fruits. The pains and sufferings of life that constantly sap the energies of all truly dedicated men and women are completely bypassed. The whole system is proposed to a theoretical humanity whose unique concern is to make the most of its physiological differences, while living in a state of radiant health and total ignorance of any form of sacrifice, atonement, or participation in the salvation of the world.

The authors of these writings assume that a relaxed and happy mood, the correct posture, the level of excitement properly rising to the pitch of orgasm constitute a completely satisfying and constantly available source of perfect pleasure. How wrong they are!

What we seek is both much more and much less. It is much more, because we see in sex, not only an emotional and physiological phenomenon, but also an expression of the deepest union of two persons, an act of love spiritualized by sacramental grace through the formal intention of the lovers. It is much less, for, being both idealistic and realistic, we are painfully aware of the limitations of the present life.

Sexual gratification is not our foremost pursuit, for in our scale of values many other things have precedence over it — many other activities which we know to be of a higher order and will inevitably decrease our physical powers. The raising of a family; any kind of dedicated work; any strenuous endeavor toward some ideal; any energy spent in assisting, counseling, sustaining the needy in body or spirit will inevitably tax our own strength and lessen our ability to reach the heights of pleasure. For we are limited in our physical and nervous means, and the more we give of ourselves to greater things outside the circle of our own welfare, the less do we have left for delight.

All this, however, is a matter of balance and measure. Ideal married life does not consist in giving so much to external activities, be they ever so lofty, that nothing is left for intimate encounters. Yet there will be many occasions when the burden of the day, increased perhaps by our own charity and generosity, will make satisfying sexual meetings completely impossible. Even such sacrifices will contribute to a couple's common ascent if properly accepted.

With libertines, the course of life, instead of being an ascending spiral that comes ever closer to the Beatific Vision, becomes a constant fall, for the senses blunted by abuse cry out for increasingly violent stimulation, leading to the multiplication of partners and to experiments in the hell-chambers of sexual aberration.

In contrast with hedonistic publications, Church-approved manuals remain so vague as to be of little use in solving practical problems of sexual adaptation and development. That is why there is an urgent need for the compilation, from a wholesome and uninhibited standpoint, of all that is healthy and valid in the literature of love, comprising detailed analyses of psychological and physiological processes. This should be made a work of art, a treasure to be cherished like the pillow-book the young Japanese bride received on her wedding night. Casting off the veils of prudery, it should make available to the newly married the full array of sexual arts developed by generations of ardent and skillful lovers — including those discoveries of refined lovemaking which many would never come to know without help; it should add to technically objective information that human quality which changes copulation into an act of love and makes of it a function of a wholesome, whole and holy rational being; it should be composed by a poet, an artist and a saint.

Young lovers should be told that success demands a rare concourse of circumstances, the right time in terms of whether a pregnancy is desired or not, the right mood and physical state in both partners, the right conditions of privacy and comfort, the right sense of deep and personal union, and finally that mysterious spark of desire which seems to come and go with the seasons and the days, and does not always coincide in husband and wife.

They should be warned that, even at its peak, sexual delight is so far from full perfection that it always leaves an aftermath of pain, be it only because it is so short. In order not to live in a state of constant disappointment and frustration, they should learn to be reconciled with such shortcomings and to practice renunciation instead of possessive greed. Instead of clinging to a pleasure they believe to be their absolute right, let them become totally free from it; instead of seeking it frantically, let them remain in peace and allow it to come to them; and let them always remember that the unexpectedness and spontaneity of truly natural desire gratefully received and generously answered leads to much higher summits than does the anxious pursuit of some impossible perfection.

Such is the book that should be written. Many eyebrows would be raised at the very thought of it, and an avalanche of criticisms and accusations of obscenity would fall on its author. And yet, the need is real and urgent, for the sexual instinct is so powerful and curiosity concerning it so keen, that if clear and complete information is not provided in the right way by the right people, the result will be either damaging ignorance or, more often, the pursuit of knowledge in the wrong way from the wrong people — and the subsequent distortion and poisoning of whole relationships. The problem, then, is not only the procuring of vital texts of poetry and literature that cover sex incidentally, but the offering of a formal and systematic treatise on a truly Christian and civilized way of love.

It is out of generosity and not unhealthy curiosity that man and wife investigate the legitimate avenues of sexual satisfaction, for it is only with the help of broad and clear information that they will be able to give each other more abundant fare than the starvation diet that leads so many marriages to a slow death. The virtuous husband is not the one who blindly trusts his natural powers, but the one who does his best to make these powers truly satisfying to his wife through intelligent and considerate selection of time, place and means; and the virtuous wife is not the one who piously and resignedly awaits the assault of the male, but the one who eagerly provokes it and makes full use of every seduction in anticipating, challenging and satisfying her husband's desire — and finds full pleasure in doing so.

On the part of the husband, inconsiderate aggressiveness and search for personal gratification at all costs are a very stupid

waste of a good thing. On the the part of the wife, mere toleration of the sexual act is an imperfection, for it is a sure sign that
something is lacking in her love, that she is unwilling to play
her full and generous part in the game. She may be hampered
by an absolutely false notion of virtue which leads her to spurn
the downright holy fun of total, naked and active surrender.

Like any form of culture, the perfect harmonization of sexual
life demands preparation and effort, which, when properly continued, bring about constant progress. Anything worth doing
is worth doing well, and of all such things the sexual adventures
of man and wife are, while perhaps the most vulnerable, the
most rewarding when properly perfected.

The man and wife relationship is both extremely simple and
supremely difficult. It is simple in that nothing is less complicated than conforming to nature, following desire all the way
until both partners are satisfied in the sexual consummation.
This is simplicity itself, the simplicity of the ideal state of two
perfect beings living in paradise. In fact, when both are weak,
imperfect, ignorant, unsure, wounded by the burden of life,
even the best of goodwill at the service of nature does not
suffice to bring about a state of blissful union. There is need of
constant and attentive perception and learning.

One of the important factors is awareness of the psychological differences between man and woman.

A man approaches sex with a ready, stable, almost constant
hunger. The only thing to spoil the fulfillment of his instinctive
drive is some external obstacle: tiredness, weakness, inhibition
or lack of opportunity. A man knows vividly that sex is good
and that he wants more of it, as soon as possible. He enjoys the
sensual memory of past experiences, and anticipates the details
of future joys. He needs no preparation, no inducement, no
change of pace: he is instantly able to drop everything for it.

A woman is entirely different. For her, sex is much more
diffuse, a part of the general pattern of tenderness and security.
She seems to have much less sensual memory: five minutes
after the wildest orgasm, she has usually forgotten all about it.

Nor are her curiosity and interest half as vivid as those of man: there is with her much less anticipation — or rather, much less detail and realism in anticipation. She may look forward with a comfortable glow to what is to come, but doesn't seem to bother about how and when. Even when fully mature and sexually awakened, she still needs to be wooed before every mating. For her, erotic pleasure is not a state into which she can fall at the drop of a slip, but the result of a more-or-less-extensive period of courting, of physical and emotional buildup. When properly warmed, she can become as ardent and active as a man, perhaps even more so, but until the right level of excitement has been reached she will have very little pleasure in receiving or in giving. The more patient and considerate the husband, the better the encounter for both.

In the protracted and tender phase of foreplay, there is more satisfying emotion, more mutual give and take, more conscious delight than in the final storm of release. The true pleasure of sex consists in this preliminary love game so often and clumsily sacrificed for the sake of immediate gratification. It may be extended surprisingly, beginning with the conspiracy of lovers holding hands or glancing at each other in the midst of a crowd, progressing to little attentions and secret communications that set the emotions aglow, building up with the evening meal as a silent symphony that drowns out the wailing and demands of children, culminating in the haven of privacy. Even then, all is not over in a flash: the glory of it may be kept going for hours — until waiting another second becomes utterly impossible!

At this point, all depends upon the proper understanding of the art of love. When husband and wife are fully prepared, aflame with desire and ready to give their all, there is still a possible mistake: both may seek to give, or even impose, what they believe the other needs. The husband may be trying to give his wife an orgasm at any cost while all she expects at the moment is tenderness and reassurance; and she in turn may be making valiant efforts to recreate some pleasure she had given in the past, instead of finding out what her husband needs right now. The true gift of self consists, not in imposing upon the partner one's own idea of an offering, but in making oneself available as an instrument to be used freely for the fulfillment of the partner's happiness, whatever it may be.

Again, it is foolish to approach sex with the intention of giving each other every time the greatest explosion of erotic ecstasy. It is much wiser to think, and even say, "I love you totally. Here I am, offered to you without reservation, as the happy instrument of any pleasure you seek at this very moment; and I am tenderly grateful to you for this same delightful service." If such offering happens to procure right now the orgasm to beat every orgasm, so be it! Alleluia! But even if it does not, there will then be no grounds for feeling frustration or disappointment.

No ceiling is imposed upon love. Since it comes about between two individuals whose worth is infinite and eternal, there are an infinite number of facets to the spiritual, emotional and physical union. That is why any dissatisfaction with married love is a sign, not that everything has been tried and rejected as unsatisfactory, but that the true savor of mutual development and possession has not been sought properly. There is no such thing as too much love leading to disgust, but too much physiological hedonism will necessarily turn into revulsion, not because sex is disgusting, but because it has been pursued in a subhuman way.

Love is in the order of action. As such, it is an art and needs to be learned and perfected. Art, according to St. Thomas, consists in doing well what needs to be done. It implies an intelligent artist, some matter upon which to work, and the proper instruments.

No art or craft or instrument has any value independent of its function and purpose. A Stradivarius is admired, not as an assemblage of wood, glue, varnish and strings, but as one of the most perfect violins ever made. And it, even so, has its full value only as an instrument in the hands of a master musician. Likewise, the human mind is great, not as an encephalic phe-

nomenon, but as that creation of God by which man is func-
tionally able to return to him in spirit. Again, sex is wonderful,
not as a physiological organ or difference of organs, but as a
function of the rational whole destined to assure procreation
and to enrich the personal lives of husband and wife. It is not
the function itself nor the instrument — it is not Priapus — that
is worthy of gratitude and praise, but God in that through sex
he has attained a twofold and important end. The means and
the urge are God-made; the proper use is left to free will. And
the part of free will is to follow the dictates of intelligence; that
is, to use the privileges of marriage with rational and physical
skills. Since we are the artists who must freely bring about in
sex all that is consistent with human dignity and eternal happiness, we may study it virtuously and test its natural variants
and possibilities within our own sacramental love life.

There are still many who would be scandalized at the notion
that the sexual life of most couples striving toward holiness
needs to be completely revitalized. Most ecclesiastic authors
seem to believe it a fact that every meeting of man and wife
automatically results in earthshaking sensuous pleasure so em-
barrassingly strong that it needs to be restrained. On the contrary, with the pains and labors of life sapping the energies of
both partners, sexual pleasure may be as elusive as the bluebird
of happiness. Many a devoted and virtuous couple, instead of
being restrained, should be *helped* to enjoy the pleasures of
their state so flippantly despised by unenlightened counselors.
In the life of a couple fully dedicated to God through constant
care for a family that needs their love, the simple fact of man
and wife being together, alone and untired, in the proper surrounding and mood and at the proper time, seems an almost
unattainable ideal. Second honeymoons, trips taken together,
even a night away from the brood may often be practically and
financially out of reach. That is where many a devoted couple
needs help in order to protect its precious and fragile relationship.

As attentive perception is needed to develop spiritual and

rational communion between the spouses, so also intelligent research and experimentation is required to develop physical love. Because of the prejudice of shame, many married couples of great goodwill are reluctant to approach the mystery of sex with the same objective simplicity as they might any other mystery. When nothing is accepted but an utterly safe routine, when whole areas of life are rejected through fear and prejudice, the result is a restricted existence in the twilight of frustration. When all brightness is excluded under the notion that it may burn, all the lights go out, and the general tone of living turns to gray. This is true of every form of adventure and personal engagement, and most particularly of sexual love.

If so many are prone to abuse what was intended for joy, that is no reason to deny what pleasure contains of elevating good. Instead of closing our hearts to delight, we should open them in full to the abundance of clean delight, making the most of what is offered, receiving with gratitude and giving with generosity.

The right physical setting for the game of love is an important element of happiness that is often overlooked. In our modern world dedicated to pleasure, it is strange that housing and furniture are so poorly adapted to sexual intimacies. Buildings are so flimsy, partitions so thin and crowding in the cities so universal that every move and whisper of lovers becomes common property and a potential source of gossip. Only the Japanese with their paper walls seem to be in a worse predicament: either they do not mind sharing their most secret moments with family and neighborhood, or they have developed a technique of silence and restraint that must be painfully hampering.

Why should love nests be built only for illegitimate meetings? Why cannot the married couple be provided with surroundings conducive to the lyrical expressions and antics of young love? Why could they not be relieved of the constant fear of being overheard? There is something quite immoral in the constant need to repress the natural song of love. A little better planning and a measure of soundproofing would go a long way in making of erotic encounters the uninhibited, lively and satisfying celebrations they should be. It is indeed a great pity, a lack of culture and a shameful indecency to confine sexual life to total darkness, dead silence and a few functional spasms — which seems to be the limit of what contemporary buildings generally allow without danger of arrest.

In our age when there is such a widespread lack of proper lodgings for the poor, when even the minimum privacy is denied to millions living in slums and shacks, it may seem improper that anyone could even think of providing himself with the luxury of extra private quarters for the sole purpose of enjoying his wife. That, however, is not the point. Social justice and personal married life are distinct problems. We all have the duty of seeing to it, within the extent of our power and circumstances, that our neighbor lives in a way compatible with human dignity. But we also have a perfect right to build our own homes according to personal needs. Considering the importance of the marital relationship, the extra money lavished on a patio, a second garage, a playroom, or a bar would have been much better spent on personal quarters for the parents: bedroom and boudoir, separated from the rest of the house by a double door, and, if possible, a private bathroom with a wide tub, and, perhaps, a miniature enclosed courtyard for sunbathing.

This leads us to an all-important point in regard to perfecting the act of love: a thorough return to nature. I do not mean that husband and wife should skip around naked in the wilderness like faun and nymph, braving mosquitoes and poison ivy — although in the absence of pests, winged or unwinged, it may be quite a lot of healthy fun. What I do mean is that they should carefully avoid the barriers and obstacles of civilized life. There is no more powerful depressant for sexual appetite than a head full of curlers, or the untouchable product of the beauty parlor. Again, a woman's long polished nails, her fear of exertion or her exaggerated daintiness may have a deadly effect on sexual love, for in it there is need of a considerable amount of natural freedom. It is not only the body that needs to be free, but also the mind and emotions, free of artificial taboos and fears. The very power that carries away the lovers may be for them a source of anguish: yet resisting the natural flow of passion may prevent them from ever attaining the full consummation of their union. There is no danger of excessive intensity: nature takes good care of itself by cutting both desire and pleasure as soon as satiety is attained.

Another important return to nature which has great erotic value is the pleasure of bathing together, in the privacy of the home, or outdoors under sun or stars.

This yearning for unfettered life, the delight of cool water and warm sunshine on bodies unhampered by clammy and constricting wraps, the feel of the morning wind on warm flesh that bristles under the rush of cold air, the headlong dive in translucent, salty, moving waters, the frolicking chase of lovers in the surf, the joyful water games; the return together to an isolated beach or shady cabana, the embrace of damp, throbbing bodies and their union in love — all that is good and healthy and holy. And yet our crowded way of life has made it all but impossible. The blame rests in part on social customs established by the prude in defense against the prurient, but also on our own frequent inability to enjoy without sin the splendor of God's creatures. Yet every man and maid united in the bond of true love have a right to dream of such moments of freedom.

Swimming nude is undoubtedly the best way to swim. Playing at midnight with liquid fire, totally naked in a warm and phosphorescent sea, is an experience never to be forgotten — and it may be enhanced a thousand times if shared with a loving playmate. Try it any time in June on the white sand shoals between Saint-Honorat and Sainte-Marguerite, if you can find the place on the map. But enough dreaming: this is supposed to be a serious book!

Nudity is not necessarily involved with sin. Many are those

who are drowned at sea: should man then cease to sail? Many are those who have sinned at the sight of nudity: should man then cease to look upon it? Sinning is no more part of nudity than drowning is part of the sea; both are accidents that befall those who venture imprudently. As the sea is the natural playground for man's spirit of adventure, so is nudity for his sexual dream.

Nudity, on the other hand, may be nothing more than an expression of natural freedom, a rejection of conventional constraint, an act of liveliness and self-assertion by which we seek a closer contact with nature. There is something purifying and elevating in the frank admission that we are of the earth, earthly, and that we enjoy it in all that it implies of healthy objectivity and uninhibited goodness. In no way does this attitude contradict our supernatural destiny: we are indeed very much on the earth, of the earth, from the earth, and this is splendid: for the earth reflects in many ways the glory that is God. We shall not gain the kingdom of heaven any the sooner for having hidden this joyful news under layers of coyness, for there is often more pride and hypocrisy in a party dress than in our original birthday suit — and God is by far the better designer.

To the pure all things are pure. And so it is with the nude body. There is no need within a loving family to cultivate prudery with cries of holy horror at every sign of overexposure: on the contrary, the sharing of home facilities within the intimacy of father, mother and children in the simplest state of nature may be an important source of later sanity. There simply is no better way for the discovery and acceptance of the difference between the sexes. Perhaps an age limit should be set — but it should not come as a sudden change of policy, as if something formerly innocent had suddenly become naughty. In most cases, even without warning, the natural reserve of loving and free children will make them modest by imperceptible degrees in exactly the right way.

Nakedness is the shameful state of being stripped of clothing;

nudity, the delightful freedom of having no need of it — and of being stripped of shame. All this is a matter of time and place, and, most of all, privacy. In warm climates, the main purpose of clothing is to preserve the sacred and personal value of the nude body; its main function is to be taken off in a gesture of total surrender and love.

The habit of nudity is quite another thing, for overexposure robs "the difference" of much of its mystery and appeal. There seems to be nothing less sexy than a nudist camp. What is too easily seen is less ardently desired. Even in the warmest and most successful marriage, total nudity must be preserved as a special gift. That is why the bikini is such a great a killer of sex appeal: it leaves too little to the imagination. What is desirable in woman is not the maximum area of exposed flesh allowed by police regulations, but that particular nudity which is the sign of the gift of herself. When there is no corresponding gift, the display of every possible bit of the skin acts as a repellent to the true lover of feminine beauty, attracting only the primate who associates desirability with exhibitionism. The bikini may at times express a true offering within the limits permitted by social customs: this offering, however, should not be made to the general public. For what is offered is a precious thing, an enchantment perhaps for the clean of heart, but also a target for the malicious eye. And since wolves outnumber the poets and the saints, we must sadly advise the pretty ones to be more discreet.

Nudity is undoubtedly natural and good in the bedroom. Stark nakedness, however, may often be improved upon, for there is great attraction in the partly veiled body and much pleasure at the sight of its progressive uncovering. The most virtuous wife may, without blushing, take full advantage of the art of strip tease, for her husband's pleasure and as a means toward a warmer consummation of their love. Anything that contributes to full sexual union is good, and the artful revelation of a wife's most precious attributes and their proper display are certainly among such things. The fact that strip tease is a common nightclub practice does not make it sinful as such, any more than lovemaking itself is made sinful by its being abused by prostitution. To restrict lovemaking to the act itself is mere puritanical obscurantism. Not only are the most extensive and exciting provocations permissible: they are *desirable* and *virtuous*. The bond of marriage is strengthened through the full and delightful game of mutual seduction every time there is a promise of a true feast of love.

Life contains so many occasions for penance and sacrifice that when, for a change and as an act of God's kindness, a moment of sheer happiness is offered to us, it would be downright stupidity and ingratitude not to make the most of it, not to drink in with holy enthusiasm every drop of wholesome, sensual, erotic pleasure it contains. If and when the romantic adventure with a beloved wife proves possible and promising, by all that is simple in heaven, let us not spoil our fun by some idiotic scruple and miss what God intended to be a soothing and reassuring ecstasy, with all its humor, its touching human quality, its emotional storm and total appeasement, its mutual giving and taking — the full satisfaction of man's most universal need. Let there be full abandon and freedom in the intensity and refinement of caresses; let there be full mutual procuring of the most intense sensual delight through the proper and natural excitation of all that is excitable in two mutually adapted bodies, one flesh by the very sacramental and sacred value of their intimacy.

In the celebration of the feast of love, let us take all the talents that God has given us and make the most of them to the limit of our art and strength, in a supremely human act that is a physical, emotional and rational expression of total love. Let us then be part of life, of the providential pattern of increase and multiplication, in the passionate way of all living things, but also in the conscious, joyful and grateful manner of God's children whom God himself has told and taught to play.

 XIX

Sex and Spirituality

"It cannot but follow that the Holy Spirit is present
during this activity." LEONARD LESSIUS

Marriage has often been seen as a symbol of the union of
Christ with the Church; it has also been compared to the
Trinity, comprising the Lover, the Beloved and their mutual
Love. In God, the dynamic interrelationship is so effective that
it is identified with the divine essence and brings forth the
Gift, the Fruit, the very Person of the Holy Spirit, the Principle of all life and love. In the union of man and woman,
created participation in the divine power brings forth their
mutual love, and also the child.

By reflecting the trinitarian principle of the universe, husband and wife are no longer limited to their personal egos:
they share in the universality of creation. Their existence begins
to make cosmic sense, their deeds take on a positive aim along
the axis of the providential plan. They move through the
boundless expanse of true freedom. Time ceases to run away
from them; now it works for them in the maturing of their
love and of its fruit. No longer do they live in a state of
anguish, counting as lost the days and years gone by; no longer
do they suffer as isolated rocks in the stream of life, tumbled
and rolled and finally drowned by forces to which they are

not permitted to yield; for they themselves have now become the water and the stream and the very source of life.

They reflect trinitarian dynamism in the wholeness of their humanity, in the fullness of their deeds. The Holy Spirit is present as the First Mover and Final End of every act of true love, even in the ecstatic consummation of the conjugal union. Narrow-minded counselors may declare that such a material union could have no spiritual value whatsoever; they may advise the spouses to abstain from it in favor of mental devotion; they may piously suggest that a good Christian couple would do better to pray together, meditate together on some holy topic or read some edifying book — any of which would in their opinions be much more virtuous than making love. In this they are dead wrong.

Their error is based on a misunderstanding of the human act. Whatever a man or woman do, they are acting as a whole with their dual nature — and not with their bodies or spirits alone. The relative merit of different acts is founded, not on their content of spirituality, but on their content of true, vital and existential love. There is, then, as much of the "spiritual" in making love rightly as there is in engaging together in some exercise of devotion — and there may even be in the former greater charity and merit.

It is a fallacy to believe that God always frowns on the game of love; after all, it was he himself who offered it to man and woman. The sexual instinct is God-made, and so are the corresponding organs, and their quality of excitability and pleasure-giving, and so also is the many-splendored delight they procure.

Every accomplishment that results in experiential ecstasy contains an element of the divine. By ecstasy, I mean what the root of the word implies: some form of going-beyond-oneself, of standing-out-above-contingency, of participating in the absolute. This occurs in any personal contact, either with God himself or with a representation of him in a creature. Thus there are mystical ecstasies binding man with God, personal ecstasies in the relationship between man and woman, and artistic ecstasies in the acts of aesthetic creation or perception. Different as they may appear at first sight, all three forms are closely related in that they all consist in dedication to a fitting object. In all three, spirit, imagination and sensuality are involved in a fusion that results in a total and gratuitous gift of self, out of which comes in return the countergift of the object sought. Ecstasy is the flowering of union in the single act of giving/receiving — and it is perfect only when its object is God.

In mystical ecstasies, this condition is fulfilled automatically since God is the object directly sought. In personal ecstasies — that is, in the consummation of marriage — the highest form of spiritual happiness appears only if the total dedication of love is made, not to the all-too-imperfect person of the partner, but to this same person as a sign and gift of God. No greedy love will ever reach this summit — be it the search for oneself through the other or the search for the other as an absolute object. For love is nothing if it is not adoration, and since we and our partners are by nature imperfect, both narcissism and romantic idealism are bound to fail.

The main objection to sexual ecstasy proposed by Scholastics in general and Thomas Aquinas in particular seems to be that it produces a temporary loss of the power of intellectual contemplation. In fact, there is no loss of any power nor anything against reason in an experience so intense that reason happens at times to be overwhelmed. If cold calculation and precise intellectual awareness were absolute conditions of virtue, every form of ecstasy would be sinful, including the highest mystical states. It is not by mere coincidence that, in their attempt to describe spiritual delights, great mystics invariably express themselves in the language of passionate love. St. Thérèse of Lisieux, in her *Autobiography*, frequently uses terms of sentimental and even physical love. In the Knox translation, however, all this has been so carefully Englished that the poor saint is made to speak in circumlocutions worthy of a Victorian prude.

There is, of course, an important difference between sexual and mystical union: sexual love seeks God through personal contact with a creature; mystical love seeks him in himself. Both, however, are communications with the reality of love. That is why mystical literature reads like a lyrical description of sexual love. This is one more proof that the latter cannot be vile, and that exaltation beyond the scope of the intellect may be good.

A full and sufficient control of sexual activity does not imply the preservation at all times of the power of rational thought. Even in our everyday life, we do not think constantly, even less do we think constantly of God. The greatest mystics are unable to keep God permanently in their conscious minds, nor is anybody expected to do so. What we need is to be aware of God as the origin and end of our being, so that all our acts are motivated by this supreme fact. Such a motivation is a matter of intention, of the will. Once the intellectual choice for God has been made, the will remains under proper guidance even without full consciousness of the motive principle.

The development of any phase of love — or of any other action — cannot possibly be accompanied by direct awareness of God for the simple reason that the intellect cannot be intent upon more than one thing at a time. Even in a placid state, it must concentrate upon what happens to be the task of the moment. It returns to God only when there is need of a free act of judgment; that is, whenever some possible good must be compared to the absolute.

A common mistake at this point is to blame the beast, to accuse the flesh of betraying the spirit. The true betrayal consists in this: we often surrender to the incomplete, to a relationship that is too shallow because it lacks the depth proposed by the Spirit of Love, because it fails to reach the level of a self-engagement proposed, not to the rational mind alone, but to the whole human being, both mind and flesh. Incongruous as it may seem to the falsely spiritual, true love implies total physical involvement with the incarnate object of carnal desire. In marriage, it is all-that-he-is seeking in the partner all-that-she-is, in the name of All-That-Is. Love play is enjoyed, not by man as a beast, but by man as a recipient of the Spirit of Love.

There is nothing low or beastly in love well played. On the contrary, its moments of exaltation and its afterglow of tender gratitude belong to the higher regions of the soul. This is indeed an occasion for rejoicing together and in each other in the name of all that is good; this is a high act of thanksgiving, fundamentally religious because it reaches for absolute Good, conforms to absolute Love and is enlightened by absolute Truth.

The game of love may be played in full, with the approval of God, as an act not of the body alone but of body, heart and soul, in the mutual ecstasy of a possession that is accepted as temporal and imperfect, but is yet a total gift of self. Love-making may be so transmuted, humanized and spiritualized in intent as to become a magnificent prayer in act — for what is prayer if not an expression of love, and what better expression of love than the supremely human surrender by which we love so overwhelmingly as to lose the consciousness of ourselves? Why not, by a rational act, see in the beloved a sign and gift of God and address to the Giver the full passion of our love for his image?

Then only will the act of love turn into absorption by what really counts, participation in the only true reality, which is Love-as-such, a reality beyond rational thought. Let us then see in human ecstasy, limited as it is in perfection, duration and object, a truthful promise of better things to come. And let us be eternally grateful for the privilege of enjoying on earth this much of paradise: the utter intimacy of two human beings, nude before each other in body and mind, and so dedicated to each other that each has no greater pleasure than to give what the other can receive and to receive what the other has to give; that game of all games of which man and woman never tire so long as they conform to the rules; that form of union of two persons delighted in the vital, providential and sacramental gift of their most sacred and reserved treasures, which procures a deep sense of suitability, of decency in the true meaning of the word, of intimate participation in the life of the cosmos.

It is this gift that shortsighted counselors would like to see dying down in the ideal couple, to be replaced by a more "spiritual" relationship. Such a view implies that sex is intrinsically opposed to the spirit. It is amusing to note that Mohammed, in contrast, advises his disciples to make love every night in order to have a clear mind in the morning.

The abuse of sex is certainly detrimental to the intellectual and spiritual life, but not more than is the abuse of anything else. Its respectful and joyful use within marriage, however, contributes substantially to the development and harmony of the whole man; and the sense of wellbeing that follows upon a happy encounter has a positive influence on any work performed while the feeling lasts.

As a couple grows to maturity, as the partners become ever closer to each other, the communion between them is intensified on every level. That is why sex must continue to play its part. The mutual attraction of manliness and femininity, which are essential qualities of the persons, must endure as a permanent factor of conjugal society. To say that physical ardor should be toned down progressively — and preferably extinguished — amounts to removing from married life a positive value that is thoroughly worth preserving. If ardor is reduced to such a low ebb in many middle-aged couples, it is not because it has yielded to some higher form of spiritual union, but because even the lesser value of physical union has been lost through ignorance or overindulgence.

The sexual urge needs to be toned down only when it becomes excessive and overwhelming; when it absorbs too much time, attention and energy in proportion to what it actually deserves. It should never be extinguished under the pretext of making a marriage more perfect. On the contrary, it should be carefully kept aflame through the avoidance of both excess and monotony.

The sense of wonder, of extraordinary privilege, before the eager and active surrender of a loving woman has no age limit: when properly fostered, it seems to grow forever and to bring with it increasing gratitude. One of the most important recipes of a happy sex life is the safeguarding of this respectful wonder, of this marveling at the mystery of love which makes of the union of two bodies so much more than a physical act. There is no romantic exaggeration here or any naïve optimism. The best things in the world are free: air, sunshine and love cannot be bought. There is the greatest wisdom, the highest degree of sophistication in the power to concentrate on such simple things in order to enjoy them in full. We may in this fashion regain part of paradise lost: that share of it that vanished, not because of the flaming sword of God's wrath, but because of the destructive power of our own scattering and unrest. Our "civilization" has become so complicated that we hardly have any time or strength left for essentials: all our energy is spent in making money to pay taxes to send astronauts to the moon — when it would have been so much simpler and more fruitful to love! Man has a right to indulge in his dreams of conquest — but not at the cost of a completely distorted sense of values. . . .

If only we could concentrate the fullness of our attention on each of the simple things we do, marveling at each gift of the earth as if it were the first, giving it as much care as if it were the last, then indeed every sunset would be the promise of a night like no other night, every dawn the promise of a day like no other day. This indeed would be wisdom. And so with love: if we only knew the gift of God and approached each love meeting as if it were the first and last, even the desert would blossom forth.

When the notion of sexual love is weeded of all its exaggerated romanticism and reconstructed in its true relationship with the divine, it becomes an important and valuable part of spiritual life. What is written here is no mere idealism or unfounded poetic rhetoric: in the sexual flowering of marriage there is solid and substantial reality sufficient to feed the deepest and most compelling hunger. Such food is never found by the children of darkness because they lack one of its principal ingredients: harmony with the Spirit of Love. But for the children of light, those who start out with open eyes and hearts pounding with expectation, the harmony of sexual union promises and provides true happiness, not that all in marriage is wine and roses, but that there is nothing which true marriage — true in that it is vital and generous — cannot overcome and turn into an occasion of sanctity.

And so, in spite of the filth and immorality of a great proportion of our modern world, in spite of displays of gross and animal sensuality and of the apparent victory of sin, there is great hope for the healthy and holy youth, for the children of light, the sons and daughters of the Holy Spirit.

We often seem to forget that all the marvels of human love are but reflections of this supreme reality, and that this Spirit is the source of all that is good in the relationship between man and woman. Many believe that there is a certain delight that can only be had on earth: they must reach for it at all costs right now, before it is too late. They fail to realize that in the Beatific Vision, in the constantly renewed and perfected act of loving perfect Love and being loved by Him, there is fully contained the enjoyment of all that is good in human love, including the delightfulness of sensual bliss. One does not marry in heaven, for there is no carnal intercourse, nor are sexual partners joined together or switched around. And yet, nothing of the joy of sexual possession could possibly be missing. On the contrary, it is there only that possession can be fully realized, becoming an exchange infinitely more intimate and satisfying than any union of physical organs.

Love in heaven will have nothing biological, but we should not believe that it will have nothing sexual, for we shall rise with our sexed bodies, and it is the whole risen complex that will be both the object and the subject of love. Union, then, shall be relieved of the burden of matter; that is, of the limitations of space and time. It will consist in seeing and holding the beloved in God by the very same act that unites lover and beloved to God. Although the Beatific Vision is universal in that, seeing God, we see all, still we shall perceive and possess with greater pleasure and intensity those who, by nature or choice, we more particularly loved in the course of our earthly pilgrimage. In that sense, true lovers shall most certainly exchange greater delights in heaven than they had ever given each other on earth.

There is in heaven both perfection and eternity in the fulfillment of marriage. The formula "until death do us part" in the wedding ceremonial is not liturgical, but merely customary and limited to a few English-speaking countries. It is misleading in that it seems to indicate a termination to the union of love. In fact, it marks the boundaries, not of the conjugal union, but of the legal and temporal tie. In no way does it forecast the separation of lovers. On the contrary, when during their lifetime two human beings have shared the most intimate form of common life, helping each other along the way to perfection through an ever-deeper dedication and understanding, it is unthinkable that such communion would not receive its crowning in a bond ever renewed and exalted in heaven.

Nothing is lost of our true loves and desires, and nothing will go unfulfilled. There is not one longing of perfect love, one fleeting vision of beauty, one surge of emotion and sorrow at the sight of some unattainable splendor that has not been recorded in the book of life. One of the joys of heaven will be the surprised encounter with the full-flowered splendor of our highest dreams, no longer in the distance, beyond grasp; no longer under the threat of loss or aging or decay: every glimpse of beauty we ever had, every fleeting ecstasy at the sight of a desired object will be fulfilled in the possession, undisturbed and unending, of the splendor we had perceived so briefly and imperfectly. Even images long past and forgotten, youthful emotions at the awakening of love, hungers long buried in the blessed soothing of time will be given back to us in full vivacity and satisfied with overflowing measure.

Heaven is no dull place of twanging harps and dusty angel wings, but of dynamic pulsing life, ever renewed and ever satisfying, the Keeping of the Promise and infinitely more. No eye has seen, nor ear heard, what is in store for the blessed of the Lord. And the reward will be all the greater for those who, in their striving toward perfect love, forfeited many an opportunity for inferior joy and premature consolation in spite of the hunger and longing in their hearts.

Plaisirs d'amour ne durent qu'un moment; chagrins d'amour durent toute la vie. Truly, the pleasures of love are soon forgotten, while the sorrows of love unfulfilled last a lifetime. In a higher sense, the valuable sorrows of love — the sacrifices imposed upon natural cravings in the name and in the hope of a higher love — will not only last until death, but will shine as jewels in our crown of glory and become the cause of joys infinitely greater than those we bypassed with soul-wrenching pain. That, and that alone, is the justification of chastity.

 **XX**

The Virtue of Sex

"The marriage act can be an act of charity."
DENIS THE CARTHUSIAN

"To know it is not so good as to love it.
To love it is not so good as to enjoy it."
CONFUCIUS

The proper use of sex, both rightful and delightful, is very much dependent upon a realistic sense of proportion. *In medio virtus.* Sex will yield its unique measure of peace, happiness and consolation — and its flashes of paradise — only when taken for what it is in truth — that is, when all scorn, fear and anguish are removed from it — and also when it is cleared of that exaltation *oltre misura* so justly condemned by Pius XII in *The Apostolate of the Midwife.* In the properly balanced contact between spouses sustained by the expectation, performance and memory of total union, there is an immeasurable wealth of virtue.

By its very nature, the act of love is one whole and continuous ascension. Once it has been set in motion, any obstacle, inhibition or slowing down tends to destroy it completely. That is why the taming and control of the senses must take the form, not of scruples within the act itself, but of an adequate orientation prior to it. Some few primitives may be able to make love and enjoy it thoughtlessly: most of us are too rational to be content with instinct alone. We need to think, to understand and justify our deeds. This understanding and justification must be achieved in advance in the clarity of the objective mind. No moral problem can be solved through direct sexual experience. If we come to this experience with anxiety, all the fun of it will be lost. If we come with the wrong answers, our whole life, temporal and eternal, may be in danger, in that we may be preparing for ourselves a future of misunderstanding with immeasurably serious consequences. As Rilke said so well, "Almost everything grave is difficult — and everything is grave"[1] — particularly in the sexual relationship.

Sex rightly used eliminates obsession, for the satisfaction of the natural drive within the norms of reason — that is, including a lavish mutual gift of sensual love — serves not as kindling for a devouring fire, but as a steady and pacifying flame that grows in warmth and quality. Wherever obsession appears, or the fire of passion rises to a dangerous heat, sex is not rightly used. The universal erotomania which is so much part of our present civilization — or of the lack of civilization — is a certain sign, not that sex has reached its full development, but that it is immature. The countless manifestations of this undeveloped state — the sexy shows, the lurid paperbacks, the playboy clubs, the pinup girls and "frank" magazines — are proof of a general sexual dissatisfaction. Such artifices are needed only as compensation for the lack of the real thing. Excessive greed and concern have turned what was to be a source of deep delight into a jungle of perversions and disappointments. The reason is precisely that sex, instead of being a virtuous habit, has become an end in itself. Instead of remaining a true but secondary reward of love, it has turned into an absolute religion. And it is this exaggeration that has robbed it of its true good.

There is a widespread tendency to accuse Christianity of

---

[1] *"Fast alles Ernste ist schwer — und alles ist ernst."* (*Briefe an einen jungen Dichter.*)

having extinguished love. The thought is expressed or implied in many works, but nowhere more precisely, perhaps, than in Jean Giono's explanation of the title of one of his novels, *Que ma joie demeure* (*Let My Joy Be Lasting*).

> As a title for my book, I have taken that of a Bach chorale, "Jesus, let my joy be lasting!" But I eliminated the first word, the most important one of the whole plea, the name of the one to whom the call is addressed, the only one who, until now, has been of importance in the search for joy; I eliminated it because it is a renunciation. We should not renounce anything. It is easy to reach inner joy by depriving ourself of our body. I feel there is greater honesty in seeking total joy, taking the body into account, since we have it, since it is there, since it is that which supports our life, from our birth to our death. To satisfy intelligence is not a difficult thing; neither is it difficult to satisfy our mind. It seems that to satisfy our body humiliates us; and yet, it alone is the bearer of a blinding knowledge.[2]

Giono, a great artist and a lover of all that is alive and beautiful, could see Christ only through Jansenistic teachings which he mistook for Christian truth. These same teachings are still abroad, and they continue to produce the same rotten fruit.

Christianity in no way limits the delight of living. On the contrary, supported by the solid realization that sacrifice is always inevitable and potentially beneficial, Christianity increases the delightfulness of all that is good, for none receive greater pleasure than those who renounce their selfish greed and seek at all times to follow the Spirit of Life.

The genuine Christian is free and joyful. Nothing is denied him but sin. If some restrictions are imposed upon his sexual activity, they do not come from Christ as a severe moralist, but from the very nature of man. Utter license leads not to the exalted summit of pleasure but to brief flashes of satisfied

[2] Translated from *Les vraies richesses* (Paris: Grasset, 1937), Preface, pp. 17-18.

lust followed by long periods of nagging despair and hunger which no amount of indulgence can appease and which may even lead to suicide.

Since man is free, he has the power to flout his nature, but not to get away with it. Human nature cannot be satisfied with anything short of absolute happiness. All of us, and rightly so, desire the best, and all of it, and right now, and forever. How could the pursuit of unrestricted erotic excitement do anything but prove that man is meant for better things?

Many who place their ultimate hope in some final and perfect revelation of sex are left after endless changes of partners to the emptiness of utter discontent. But those who do seek the absolute as it should be sought, and in the course of their pilgrimage meet a companion to share their dream of paradise, have every good reason to walk joyfully in their love. They shall receive as a true and holy gift the ecstasies of mutual possession and ever-deepening discovery. Every person is a fountain of infinity, and when love rises to drink of this personal source, there is always available a more generous giving and a more grateful receiving. Man and wife can then rejoice in their spirit as their flesh perceives pleasure, for they are then whole and one within the bond of their love.

The golden firebird of love is never caught by greedy hands. It burns to death those who would make of it a god. It sears the flesh of the lustful and enslaves those who bow to its excessive demands. But, like the phoenix, it rises again and again in glory for those who truly love.

The French poet Edmond Rostand composed in *Chantecler* these beautiful lines to the glory of the sun:

> *Soleil, O toi sans qui les choses*
> *Ne seraient que ce qu'elles sont!*
> (Sun, O you without whom all things
> Would be no more than what they are!)

The same may be said of love, but in a much deeper sense. Life enlightened with true love glows with glorious sunshine, for love gives a special brilliance and glitter to the moments of our joy.

Since all love is art, the supreme Lover is the supreme Artist, the origin and model of all beauty. Love is truly art in that it brings out splendor and glory, that it adds to reality the spark of delight which may be struck from every created thing because everything comes from the hand of supreme Delight. Love is not only art, but poetic art in the full sense of the word and in its original meaning, for love is a matter of action, of doing. The poet is the man who acts out his inner vision, the man of truth and fire, the man without half measure or compromise, the man who would rather die than abandon his pursuit. Poet and lover always meet, for they have a common goal: Galatea. Both pursue perfection and seek to make it live; and they are truly one, for in the poet the lover sings, and in the lover the poet does his deed.

The poet in us may dream of different climes, of worlds of ease and contentment in which there would be no tiredness or pain, where our own true love would rise like Venus from the sea with the grace and promise of a Tahitian maiden, cool and dripping in the breeze. We may suffer from a feeling of regret for all we missed, for the many unattainable splendors of the passing world escaping forever from our grasp, for the moments of sweet passion that never came to be, for the sun so seldom shining over blissful communications of love.

How much is valid in such longing and regrets? They may be seen as veiled images of our desire for perfect love, for that Person who is the perfection of love, the most holy Spirit who breathes both life and love in all that is living and loving.

> We could not be fundamentally and inexhaustibly happy without our being becoming personally united with something personal in the ALL. Fundamentally, that is what is called "Love." [3]

[3] Teilhard de Chardin, quoted by Mrs. Parry-Hausenstein in *Search* (London: Michael de la Bedoyere, April 1964), p. 462.

Sexuality is the stuff such dreams are made of. It is found not only in the union of bodies but in the way we think and live. It is a dynamic and vital force that definitely helps the world go round. It adds tremendous emotional value to our days by raising us to a dimension of gratuity and surprise that may far exceed the rewards of intellectual creation. T. S. Eliot would seem to be at least one great contemporary poet who abruptly ceased to write as soon as he began to live his love. This was no loss, at least to him, for there is more poetical value in the actual love of a man for a woman than in the sum total of amorous literature. Conversely, it is the poet's despair to be unable to render in words anything of the glory of his love. Broken hearts can gush forth a stream of sorrowful verse; few poets can sing delight. The language of love is silence; its act is playful and childlike consent.

Perfect love no longer exists on earth. Perhaps it never did. Perhaps it is no more than a dream of infinitude in minds created for an infinite Love that so transcends any earthly paradise as to make even the groves of Eden seem too cold. And yet, there is in the glory of man-with-woman a height that comes closer to perfect happiness than could anything else:

> Lenny opened her arms. For the first time in my life I saw what I knew existed, the fullness of a person, the space that rises up around us into the extraordinary air and light and the height that has no end, the fullness that inhabits the earth and gives it a voice, that forces itself to be heard and that exists in itself, which is all the universe must be, and if there is more, it can only be of the same, but we don't know, and that is why we live, and that is why our voice is never still.[4]

It is a rare treat to discover in the words of another a perfect expression of our own faith. There is here beautifully expressed a sacred verity, a shared secret, the fruit of a mysterious initia-

[4] *Can I Get There by Candlelight*, Julius Horwitz (New York: Atheneum, 1964), pp. 218-219.

tion obtained in the flames of brilliant and successful love. Those who enjoy it radiate peace, rejoice in each other and cannot stop singing their gratitude for the mutual gift.

The context of this quotation is of little import: it may be taken as a gem in its own right, a spontaneous and deep expression of one man's true sense of love, so convincing that it becomes a universal truth.

It is hard to tell exactly how and when a sexual union flowers into something absolutely superior to the partners in the game.

> There must be two in one, always two in one — the sweet love of communion and the fierce, proud love of sensual fulfillment, both together in one love. And then we are like a rose. We surpass even love, love is encompassed and surpassed. We are two who have a pure connection. We are two, isolated like gems in our unthinkable otherness. But the rose contains and transcends us, we are one rose, beyond.[5]

Lovers are touched by a magic that may contain a natural lure leading to the reproduction of the species. Yet, there is here something infinitely superior to the instinctive urge, something truly elevating, a divine folly of mutual dedication and sacrifice, a direct contact with that reality which is the essence of the universe.

Few things are of greater and rarer beauty than interpersonal harmony. Friendship and love are the stuff heaven is made of. In a sense, friendship may be the higher because it is the more detached, but in the existential reality of the human person no possible relationship can attain the height and closeness experienced by a loving couple. Their sexual contacts, while not the only manifestations of love, account for something totally irreplaceable, a joyful conspiracy, a connivance of two bodies doing well what they were made to do in the mutual

[5] *Sex, Literature and Censorship*, D. H. Lawrence. Essays edited by Harry T. Moore (New York: Twayne, 1953), p. 37.

and secret surrender of their all. Love of friendship, platonic love, intellectual companionship, all these may be maintained on a high and rewarding plane. Yet they suffer from a streak of unfulfillment, a threat of neurotic pitfalls, a lack of complete humanity. For mankind is male and female, and nothing but the union of the sexes can satisfy the hunger for love on earth. In this union, there is the humble recognition of individual insufficiency, a cry from the abyss of loneliness, a longing for a perfection as yet unknown — every one a sign and symbol of the Beatific Vision. In the beloved, the lover sees, in the reality of the here and now, the rainbow hues of the covenant with God, for the relationship with the beloved is a prelude to that relationship in which we live and are and have our being.

What is it that gives to a sexual encounter that unmistakable flavor of paradise which, once perceived, leaves an unquenchable longing for more? There are so many conditions to perfect — or near-perfect — love that it is a task of the utmost delicacy to unravel and analyze its threads. Who will know whether the conditions are the same, or even comparable, for two distinct couples, both of which feel they have attained the height of happiness?

The quality of satisfaction is dependent upon the refinement and development of desire, the truly sensitive needing a much higher degree of harmony than the simply sensual. Perhaps sexual happiness is much harder for the poet and saint than it is for the less cultured and demanding, since the former will expect much more. He is far from content with the physical storm, its ecstasy and relief; he seeks unutterable contact of the person in the most intimate exchange of love. The physical conditions are commonly attainable; they imply only the co-operation of healthy bodies. But how and where and when shall the poet find his love fulfilled? Only by special grace shall he find his mate.

Is an encounter of such quality the privilege of a few favored lovers, a chance concordance of two propitious strains, a natural miracle comparable to the evolutionary leap that brings forth a new and more richly fragrant blossom? It appears rather as the ever-fresh reflowering of one of the most ancient blooms on the vine of redeemed humanity, a triumph of life eternally renewed.

A truly satisfactory sexual celebration is a tremendous victory of the person. It is a victory over the harshness of daily reality, over the pressure of competition, over feminine reserve, over one's own self-doubts and inhibitions. It is also a hard-won victory over the many artificial obstacles placed before our hopes and dreams by an educational approach that is so often wrong, consisting as it does in warnings and prohibitions.

No other situation or action offers so direct a participation in the forces of the earth, so much sharing in what is both the most personal and universal function of man — that by which he becomes an active link in the chain of life, the recipient of countless generations and the potential ancestor of countless others. There may be no awareness of all this in the performance of the act of love: lovers may even be offended at the thought that their love is not unique. In this they are partly right, for sex is a common experience only in terms of biology and psychology. In terms of existential living, each experience is totally new. Each meeting of man and woman, like every dawn and every passing of the tide, has a character of utter originality, a primeval perfection ever reborn. For each encounter of lovers is creation played anew. And yet this newness of dawn and tide and love is but the daughter of millions of renewals; and what makes their newness possible today is the pulse of countless centuries.

"There are more things in heaven and earth, Horatio, than are dreamt of in your philosophy," and in your love there is the blind memory of a million matings, the unconscious participation in a living reality which exceeds by far any perception of the past. It is in the combination of these two elements — our acutely existential reality and the tremendously deep strata from which we rise — that we find both the roots of our sexual desires and the pacifying notion that, when they are being satisfied, we are participating directly in the dynamic order of life.

Ageless, then, is the game of man and woman; ageless their mutual challenge, their desire to seduce each other by word or deed, by dress or by the lack of it, by their complete attitude toward each other when sex is in season. It is in response to an ancestral urge that each must court and provoke the other, while also being courted and provoked by the other, so that they can meet and mate in the unity of their mutual desire. At such times — and it has always been so — modesty and reserve are wrong, and so is impatience and greed, for they tend to deprive both partners of their fun, of what was made to be the supreme form of adult play, the best remedy to sadness, isolation and despair; an act of immense human and divine significance. There is no better time for the singing of psalms than the morning after a night of love.

Conclusion

"Maiden, where do you go shading your lamp
with your mantle? My house is all dark and lone-
some — lend me your light."

RABINDRANATH TAGORE

The purpose of this life is to seek God in the works of creation
and to return them to him after marking them with the stamp
of love. God made nothing but what is good, so that all that
God made may be returned to him as an acceptable offering.
Between the taking and the offering, however, there must come
about a mysterious transmutation which changes the elements
of matter into spiritual gifts.

In what God made, there is nothing unclean. Some things
God made are indirect means of love; others are by nature its
very instruments. Such are the physical, affective and intellectual forms of individual expression: the power to pray to
God and to praise him; the power to seek, understand and
communicate his truth; the power to love and to live; and the
power to reproduce life. All these powers God granted for no
other reason than to bring oneness among men, the dynamic
and creative oneness of the Father, the Son and the Holy
Spirit in the perfect communication of truth and goodness.
Now, in the order of life, God so organized humanity that its
conservation and increase would be the fruit of the deepest

and most intimate communication of love, of the total mutual gift of lovers overwhelmed by their participation in the creative act.

Passion, then, far from being a distortion brought about by sex, is a primary condition of love. The Lord once said to Catherine of Siena: "All my saints are passionate! I permitted passion, and still do, for the sake of the growth of grace and the progress of virtue in souls."[1] And passion, in the sense of total, unconditional surrender to the forces of true love, is a virtue which finds a fitting expression in the procreative act.

Nonpassionate love always falls short of perfection, for there is in any restraint, in any limitation, a lack of confidence, a lack of childlikeness. As a child involves itself totally in anything it does, so do lovers engage their whole beings, body and soul, in the complete range of their pains and pleasures. Only in that are they true to each other, true to their vocation and true to their God.

What makes passion good is precisely the mysterious transmutation by which man alone is able to change matter into spiritual gifts in the furnace of love. And what makes passion evil is the absence of love: pleasure sought, not for the glory of the gift offered and received in the name of love, but for the satisfaction of cold and selfish greed.

As a flowering of true love, passion knows no limit. There is always more to give and more to receive because what is given and received in the name of love takes on a flavor of infinity. Not that any human love could ever reach perfect delight, but that it may be offered as an anticipation of perfect delight, with the clear knowledge that uncreated good contains the fullness of what is but glimpsed through the gates of earthly bliss.

Seek and you shall find. Seek passion as an end, and all you shall find is all that it can give: imperfect and fleeting pleasure. But seek the full perfection of uncreated good, and in the

---

[1] Cf. *Le dialogue de Ste. Catherine de Sienne*, M. J. Hurtaud, O.P. (Paris: Lethielleux, 1913, reprinted 1940), p. 119.

passion of your search, and in the passion of your love, everything shall turn into signs and symbols and become a foretaste
of that one reality which is all-sufficient and all-satisfying, God,
the Author of all delight.

If in our love we find the traces of supreme Love, if we
seek these traces as moments of divine tenderness supporting
us along the way, every instant of valid human passion may
be received with gratitude and joy as a proof of true and vital
participation in the dynamism of creation.

God knows what we need; and when he gives us moments
of utter joy that seem to make us partake in full of the abundance of his bounty, it would be not only utter folly but plain
ingratitude to see in them anything but clean and proper and
holy gifts. It is our spirit that has the power of changing blind
instinct into human glory, of elevating the physiological function to the level of ideal offering, of transmuting the embrace
of two bodies into an expression of holy love. Holy it is, for
it comes from the All-Holy; holy it is, for it is a condition of
the multiplication of saints; holy it is, for when properly used
it becomes a powerful means of sanctification. It sanctifies in
every one of its aspects: through hope for love still to come,
through gratitude for love satisfied, through sacrifices in so
many instances of love unfulfilled because we do not live in
paradise.

This love, then, may be seen as part of the universal dispen-
sation, as one particular aspect of Christ, for it is closely related
to him by its very essence, and also by the effect it brings about,
creation by participation — which consists not only in the bringing forth of children, but also in the flowering of the powers
and resources of man through woman and of woman through
man. For in their relationship there is a vibrant and living
motive-principle that gives birth to many forms of beauty.
The beloved is the proximate reason, the inspiration without
which many a masterpiece, many a deed of valor and virtue
would never have come to be. The beloved, also, is the tangible
and existential sign of the perfect Beloved toward whom every

spirit tends. Lovers on earth may find in each other more than a mere reflection of Him, for they participate in the creative principle of the cosmos made by that very Lover for the sake of love. They are real in the measure in which they develop their personal love and realize its true nature by letting it rise toward God and expand in the communion of saints. When such powers are exalted to their true heights, lovers can no longer remain silent: they must sing their joy and express it in many ways. They must fulfill their love in the exuberance of lyrical praise, in silent prayer and contemplation, in the breathtaking intimacies of bodies and minds; they must play with childlike earnestness like King David dancing before the Ark; they must bring the whole universe into their arms and make it shimmer with the stardust of delight.

"At the root of every virtue, there is a magnificent and royal lightheartedness." [2] Indeed, some things are much too important to be taken seriously: they must be accepted in a spirit that eliminates solemn ritual and rational analysis. One such is the game of love: a combination of respect, tenderness, humor, imagination, vitality and total freedom. The precious moments of love are to be lived with the utter spontaneity of life itself that follows the laws of the whole human complex, and not of the mind alone, thus producing superabundant harmony without stopping at every bar to make sure of the tune.

Few biblical images are more delightful than that of Wisdom playing before the Father at the time of creation:

When he established the heavens, I was there . . .
Playing before him all the while,
Playing on the surface of his earth . . .
(Proverbs 8:27, 30-31)

Wisdom, identified with the Word or perfect Artist, plays on the surface of the earth in the complete freedom of perfect

---

[2] Cf. *La prière de toutes les heures*, Pierre Charles, S.J.

love. Wisdom does not philosophize, analyze or synthesize: it simply plays. Wisdom does not worry about other worlds or other creations: it rejoices in this universe as it is, for it is good.

We, alas, through Adam, have spoiled it in part, and much of the spirit of childlike play has been taken away from us; much toil and labor and anguish has been added in its stead. But all spirit of joy, all spirit of spontaneous happiness has not vanished forever. No longer is it the bread of each day. Yet it does appear as a rare and elusive wonder on those occasions which combine inner peace with some surplus of vital energy left over from the labor of living. Then only can we play: when all is well with our spiritual, emotional and physical condition; then only can we play the greatest game of all, the game of man with woman and of woman with man, without restriction or worry but with utter freedom, without solemnity or fear but with utter delight.

When the precious concurrence of mood and circumstances offers true promise, let us protect our love against the prophets of gloom. Let us love with sweet madness and enjoy it in full; let us love with art and ardor, with imagination and fire; let us love with every one of our mental, physical and psychical powers in a spirit of gratefulness toward the Creator of all good things, for it is he who speaks in the Song of Songs:

DRINK DEEP, BELOVED!

Never spurn the flesh: kiss it as you would the land of your birth and of your homecoming, for it is the fruitful soil from which you spring, the bearer of what will remain of you in your children, and a part of your future resurrection. Never spurn the flesh, for you may be spurning the incarnate Christ.

Nativity, 1965

Reading List

Since the present work is not a compilation, but a study based on personal experience occasionally supported by references, there is no need for a formal bibliography. I believe, however, that the following list of titles will be useful as a guide to supplementary reading.

BIRMINGHAM, William (editor): *What Modern Catholics Think About Birth Control*, New York, Signet, 1965.

Catholic men and women discuss the Church's stand on birth control, and tell why they agree or disagree, sometimes with moving and passionate arguments.

CHESSER, Eustace, M.D.: *Love Without Fear*, New York, Signet, 1954.

A classical manual of sexual love, beginning with a psychological study of true interpersonal relationship between spouses.

FORD, John C., S.J., and KELLY, Gerald, S.J.: *Contemporary Theology*, Volume II, "Marriage Questions," Westminster, Md., Newman, 1963.

An intelligent presentation of the official position of the Church prior to Vatican II.

KERNS, Joseph E., S.J.: *The Theology of Marriage*, New York, Sheed & Ward, 1964.

A richly documented study that constitutes an eloquent if

unintended indictment of the clerical-celibate attitude toward
sex and marriage.

LAWRENCE, D. H.: *Sex, Literature and Censorship*, New York,
Twayne Publishers, 1953.
A series of articles on sex and love, written between 1928
and 1936. Some illuminating and liberating views by a con-
troversial pioneer.

NOONAN, John T., Jr.: *Contraception — A History of Its Treatment by the Catholic Theologians and Canonists*, Cambridge,
Mass., The Belknap Press of Harvard University Press, 1965.
An indispensable collection of documents of great scholarly
interest, treated with remarkable objectivity and restraint,
clearly showing the growth of the Church's doctrine from the
first century to the present, the forces shaping it and its poten-
tiality for development.

NOVAK, Michael (editor): *The Experience of Marriage*, New
York, Macmillan, 1964.
Thirteen personal stories giving a faithful description of
actual problems in the sexual lives of couples of widely different
backgrounds.

PLANQUE, Daniel: *The Theology of Sex in Marriage*, Notre
Dame, Ind., Fides, 1962.
An excellent introduction to the true values of sexuality by a
Belgian priest related to the Family Movement.

ROBERTS, Archbishop Thomas D.: *Contraception and Holiness*,
New York, Herder & Herder, 1964.
A series of articles from the conservative to the disgruntled,
following an introduction by the outspoken British archbishop.

RAINER, Jerome and Julia: *Sexual Pleasure in Marriage*, New
York, Messner, 1959.

An enlightening contemporary view on the proper sexual relationship between husband and wife, with an appendix comprising a short encyclopedia of sex guidance and information.

RAINER, Jerome and Julia: *Sexual Adventure in Marriage,* New York, Messner, 1965.
A more advanced and sophisticated guide to the enjoyment of married life, in the context of a personalistic relationship, followed by an appendix of historical interest consisting in a series of literary excerpts. The latter are not presented as examples of the proper use of sex, but merely as examples of classical writing on the subject.

ROBINSON, Marie N., M.D.: *The Power of Sexual Surrender,* New York, Signet, 1959.
A compassionate and helpful study of female frigidity and its remedies, leading to the flowering of sexual life and love.

ROCK, John, M.D.: *The Time Has Come,* New York, Avon, 1964.
This book discusses frankly, fully and fearlessly the possibilities of approved scientific birth control methods. Written by one of the scientists who developed "the pill," it presents all the evidence in favor of it.

SUENENS, Leon Joseph Cardinal: *Love and Control,* Westminster, Md., Newman, 1962.
An exposition of the traditional view of the Church, tempered by great understanding of human needs and a deep respect for the sexual relationship.

Index

247

A HAWTHORN BOOK